JOHNNIE TO KEI-FUNG'S

PTU

Hong Kong University Press thanks Xu Bing for writing the Press's name in his Square Word Calligraphy for the covers of its books. For further information, see p. iv.

THE NEW HONG KONG CINEMA SERIES

The New Hong Kong Cinema came into existence under very special circumstances, during a period of social and political crisis resulting in a change of cultural paradigms. Such critical moments have produced the cinematic achievements of the early Soviet cinema, neorealism, the *nouvelle vague*, and the German cinema of the 1970s and, we can now say, the New Hong Kong Cinema. If this cinema grew increasingly intriguing in the 1980s, after the announcement of Hong Kong's return to China, it is largely because it had to confront a new cultural and political space that was both complex and hard to define, where the problems of colonialism were uncannily overlaid with those of globalism. Such uncanniness could not be caught through straight documentary or conventional history writing: it was left to the cinema to define it.

Has the creative period of the New Hong Kong Cinema now come to an end? However we answer the question, there is a need to evaluate the achievements of Hong Kong cinema. This series distinguishes itself from the other books on the subject by focusing in-depth on individual Hong Kong films, which together make the New Hong Kong Cinema.

Other titles in the series

Andrew Lau and Alan Mak's *Infernal Affairs – The Trilogy*
by Gina Marchetti

Fruit Chan's *Durian Durian* by Wendy Gan

John Woo's *A Better Tomorrow* by Karen Fang

John Woo's *The Killer* by Kenneth E. Hall

King Hu's *A Touch of Zen* by Stephen Teo

Mabel Cheung Yuen-ting's *An Autumn's Tale* by Stacilee Ford

Stanley Kwan's *Center Stage* by Mette Hjort

Tsui Hark's *Zu: Warriors From the Magic Mountain*
by Andrew Schroeder

Wong Kar-wai's *Ashes of Time* by Wimal Dissanayake

Wong Kar-wai's *Happy Together* by Jeremy Tambling

JOHNNIE TO KEI-FUNG'S
PTU

Michael Ingham

Hong Kong University Press
14/F Hing Wai Centre
7 Tin Wan Praya Road
Aberdeen
Hong Kong

ISBN 978-962-209-919-7

British Library Cataloguing-in-Publication Data
A catalogue record for this book is available from the British Library.

Secure On-line Ordering
http://www.hkupress.org

Printed and bound by Pre-Press Ltd., Hong Kong, China

Hong Kong University Press is honoured that Xu Bing, whose art explores the complex themes of language across cultures, has written the Press's name in his Square Word Calligraphy. This signals our commitment to cross-cultural thinking and the distinctive nature of our English-language books published in China.

"At first glance, Square Word Calligraphy appears to be nothing more unusual than Chinese characters, but in fact it is a new way of rendering English words in the format of a square so they resemble Chinese characters. Chinese viewers expect to be able to read Square Word Calligraphy but cannot. Western viewers, however are surprised to find they can read it. Delight erupts when meaning is unexpectedly revealed."
— Britta Erickson, *The Art of Xu Bing*

Contents

Series Preface

The New Hong Kong Cinema came into existence under very special circumstances, during a period of social and political crisis resulting in a change of cultural paradigms. Such critical moments have produced the cinematic achievements of the early Soviet cinema, neorealism, the *nouvelle vague*, the German cinema in the 1970s and, we can now say, the recent Hong Kong cinema. If this cinema grew increasingly intriguing in the 1980s, after the announcement of Hong Kong's return to China, it was largely because it had to confront a new cultural and political space that was both complex and hard to define, where the problems of colonialism were overlaid with those of globalism in an uncanny way. Such uncanniness could not be caught through straight documentary or conventional history writing; it was left to the cinema to define it.

It does so by presenting to us an urban space that slips away if we try to grasp it too directly, a space that cinema coaxes into existence by whatever means at its disposal. Thus it is by eschewing a narrow idea of relevance and pursuing disreputable genres like melodrama, kung fu and the fantastic that cinema brings into view something else about the city which could otherwise be missed. One classic example is Stanley Kwan's *Rouge*, which draws on the unrealistic form of the ghost story to evoke something of the uncanniness of Hong Kong's urban space. It takes a ghost to catch a ghost.

In the New Hong Kong Cinema, then, it is neither the subject matter nor a particular set of generic conventions that is paramount. In fact, many Hong Kong films begin by following generic conventions but proceed to transform them. Such transformation of genre is also the transformation of a sense of place where all the rules have quietly and deceptively changed. It is this shifting sense of place, often expressed negatively and indirectly — but in the best work always rendered precisely in (necessarily) innovative images — that is decisive for the New Hong Kong Cinema.

Has the creative period of the New Hong Kong Cinema come to an end? However we answer the question, there is a need now to evaluate the achievements of Hong Kong cinema. During the last few years, a number of full-length books have appeared, testifying to the topicality of the subject. These books survey the field with varying degrees of success, but there is yet an almost complete lack of authoritative texts focusing in depth on individual Hong Kong films. This book series on the New Hong Kong Cinema is designed to fill this lack. Each volume will be written by a scholar/critic who will analyse each chosen film in detail and provide a critical apparatus for further discussion including filmography and bibliography.

Our objective is to produce a set of interactional and provocative readings that would make a self-aware intervention into modern Hong Kong culture. We advocate no one theoretical position; the authors will approach their chosen films from their own distinct points of vantage and interest. The aim of the series is to generate open-ended discussions of the selected films, employing diverse analytical strategies, in order to urge the readers towards self-reflective engagements with the films in particular and the Hong Kong cultural space in general. It is our hope that this series will contribute to the sharpening of Hong Kong culture's conceptions of itself.

In keeping with our conviction that film is not a self-enclosed signification system but an important cultural practice among similar others, we wish to explore how films both reflect and inflect culture. And it is useful to keep in mind that reflection of reality and reality of reflection are equally important in the understanding of cinema.

Ackbar Abbas
Wimal Dissanayake

Acknowledgements

I wish to acknowledge the kind support and assistance, valuable encouragement and shrewd insight of the following in the process of writing and publication of this book:

A.N. Other (my anonymous manuscript reviewer); Ackbar Abbas; Bing Baraoidan; Sharon Chan; Colin Day; Michael Duckworth; John Elsom; Shan Ding; Mette Hjørt; Dawn Lau; Gina Marchetti; Meaghan Morris; Daisy Ng; Tiffany Ng; Jean-Michel Sourd; Stephen Teo; Johnnie To Kei-fung; Kate Whitehead; Jessica Yeung; Yvonne Young; Xu Xi.

They have all been instrumental in the writing and publication of this volume, whether wittingly or unwittingly, and I am greatly indebted to them. Working on any kind of writing project can be a very solitary business, so I feel extremely fortunate to have benefited from their experience and assistance. For some, their valuable contribution is manifest in the book itself, while for others the generosity of their contribution is less obvious, but their kindness and expertise are equally appreciated. Any omissions, oversights or inadequacies in the final text are mine alone; their various contributions to the project as a whole have been exclusively benign in influence and outcome. Colin Day and Michael Duckworth at Hong Kong University Press have exercised an unfailingly benevolent, though constructively critical, supervision of the production of the manuscript and boosted morale when most needed, while at the same time knowing intuitively when to leave well alone. I cannot thank them both enough. Johnnie To's sometimes cryptic but always stimulating comments in relation to *PTU* during the interview he so kindly gave me helped to kick-start my writing, spurred on as I was by his canny but passionate approach to cinema. Finally I would like to extend my thanks to the people (personally unknown to me) who collaborated on the film production of *PTU* for their share in producing this small gem of a movie. No matter how many times I watched, I always found some formal or aesthetic detail to add to my enjoyment of the film.

1

Introducing the Film; Introducing Johnnie — 'One of Our Own'

'It is not enough to think about Hong Kong cinema simply in terms of a tight commercial space occasionally opened up by individual talent, on the model of auteurs in Hollywood. The situation is both more interesting and more complicated.'

— Ackbar Abbas, *Hong Kong Culture and the Politics of Disappearance*

'Yet many of Hong Kong's most accomplished films were made in the years after the 1993 downturn. Directors had become more sophisticated, and perhaps financial desperation freed them to experiment ... The golden age is over; like most local cinemas, Hong Kong's will probably consist of a small annual output and a handful of films of artistic interest. Nonetheless, the films that stand out will probably display an unswerving appeal to the norms and forms of popular cinema.'

— David Bordwell, *Planet Hong Kong — Popular Cinema and the Art of Entertainment*

> 'The police and criminals are different sides of the same coin. Where there are thieves, there are police. Where there are police, there are thieves. You cannot have one without the other.'
> — Johnnie To, Interview on DVD version of *PTU*

Background: Johnnie To and contemporary Hong Kong cinema

Johnnie To Kei-fung has been an unobtrusive but prolific and innovative contributor to the Hong Kong cultural scene. He is an increasingly esteemed filmmaker in Hong Kong, admired among overseas aficionados of Hong Kong action films, as well as a highly experienced film producer and the creative heart of the independent film company, Milkyway Image. However he has shunned the short-lived 'bubble reputation' of celebrity, relying rather on his prodigious work ethic and his impressive track record to do the talking for him. As well as being a key figure in the industry, To has been a member of the Hong Kong Arts Development Council, advising conscientiously and insightfully on cinema as an art form. While he has yet to enjoy the same sort of international critical acclaim as Hong Kong filmmakers like Wong Kar-wai and John Woo or transnational Chinese directors like Ang Lee and Zhang Yimou, To has commanded respect and admiration for both the variety of his output and his increasingly accomplished direction. His films continue to win recognition, both in Hong Kong's own local film awards and in European festivals.

Despite the local and international critical plaudits for *The Mission* (1999), *Running Out of Time* (1999), *PTU* (2003), *Breaking News* and *Throw Down* (both 2004), his more recent films *Election I* and *II* (2005/2006), *Exiled* (2006) and *Sparrow* (2008) and his consistent cinema work across a number of popular film genres, To has not as yet attracted quite the cachet of 'coolness' of a John Woo or a Wong Kar-wai in the broader consciousness of international film commentary. However, there is no doubt that his profile as a director is getting stronger with each passing year, and every new release, especially those in the gangster-cop genres, serves to consolidate this growing reputation. His earlier comedy and action-based genre films established his presence on the scene as an extremely competent director, and one capable of shooting a film within budget and according to schedule, both of which are crucial considerations in the frenetic, profit-margin-conscious Hong Kong film industry. For this reason To has never been anything but busy as a director and producer, frequently juggling up to three films in any given year. Just glancing at his extensive filmography, we appreciate his outstanding contribution to Hong Kong's film and television output. Yet it is only in the current decade that he has matured into a major Asian cineaste, and his films have come to suggest a distinctive, if quirky, aspect of Hong Kong's dichotomous local/global psyche, as manifest in the films of many of the city's 'New Wave' of directors. Not that To himself can really be considered a part of this new wave, despite the fact that he has played an increasingly significant part in making Hong Kong films a recognisable product in the international market-place. His name is rarely mentioned in connection with any particular grouping outside his own Milkyway enterprise.

In a 2004 essay Esther Cheung and Jamie Ku tackle this thorny issue of whether or not it is appropriate to categorise Hong Kong directors as 'New Wave', pointing out that Hong Kong cinema 'has gained the *status* of a national cinema in the film institution although Hong Kong films can by no means be understood within the paradigm of the nation-state. Some critics have been dismissive of the New Wave Cinema by questioning whether the cinema had ever existed; nonetheless a retrospective study is in fact an assertion of the New Wave and its relevance to the local and global institutional status of the Hong Kong cinema'.[1] Whilst this validation of the study of Hong Kong cinema is no doubt a compelling one, it is not exactly clear where To, as an independent figure not associated with any particular 'wave', fits into the bigger picture. Ackbar Abbas has recently posited Hong Kong's relationship with the bigger picture in his essay on Hong Kong cinema, an essay anthologised in a study of cinema of small nations. He refers to its fragmentary nature thus: 'The fragment as nation allows us to define, tentatively, in what sense it is possible to think about the Hong Kong cinema as a "national" cinema: in the sense that it is a cinema that perceives the nation from the point of view of the fragment. Its relation to nationhood is unorthodox. It does not see the nation as a finished or achieved entity, but catches it at a moment when the nature of nationhood itself is changing, under pressure from globalisation.'[2] Furthermore, in his Hong Kong cultural overview *Chinese Face-Off* Lo Kwai-cheung has referred to Hong Kong cinema's tendency to ignore the conventional paradigms of local and national by appearing to position itself independently: 'Hong Kong films made during the transitional period and even the post-97 productions are actually becoming more transnationalised than nationalised, offering a provocative reconception of what we usually mean by "local" and inadvertently subverting the concept of nation.'[3] Chu Yiu Wai, critiquing 'the seemingly pure local identity' of Hong Kong portrayed in certain post-97 films, has pointed out that this supposedly 'local' identity 'has to be problematized before any formation of identity can be negotiated in the age of transnationalism'.[4]

These perspectives on Hong Kong cinema in general are highly illuminating. However, To's name rarely comes up in the context of such critical discussion. As regards narratives of Chineseness, of diaspora or of transnational, global identity, his work does not seem to be part of any school, trend or movement, or of direct significance to such debates, as, for example, the output of directors like Ann Hui and Fruit Chan has been. Likewise he appears reluctant to involve himself in any cinematic discourse on postcolonial, post-handover identity politics, at least in terms of clarifying a stance or ideological position, although certain of his films hint at his distrust of official versions of Hong Kong–mainland relations. In any case, as we shall see in connection with the narrative symbolism of *PTU*, To is neither celebrating nor seriously exploring the relationship with mainland China, despite the fact that there is a mainland 'foreign element' embedded in the film's plot and sub-text. For all of these reasons it is difficult to cast To in the role of ardent champion of Hong Kong's local identity cause, or as a local (or glocal) hero resisting assimilation into the wider national and transnational contexts of the industry for all his Hong Kong local-boy-made-good credentials. What we can see in many of his films is a sense of marginalisation or polarisation arising from social and personal crises or contingencies. Few commentators, though, have considered his work an exemplar of theoretical-critical paradigms in respect of Hong Kong postcoloniality. One of the aims of this study is to assess whether, in fact, it does have something astute to say about Hong Kong's postcolonial identity.

To a considerable extent Stephen Teo's detailed new critical study of To's career, *Director in Action — Johnnie To and the Hong Kong Action Film*, has helped to address the paucity of critical assessment of his work to date. Indeed, Teo's informed and insightful account of his development as a major, contemporary Asian filmmaker has filled a gaping lacuna in contemporary Hong Kong film studies, and his identification of To as 'an uneven auteur' offers us a critical yardstick to explore his work further. This critical evaluation will be explored more closely in the concluding chapter in connection with the film's 'aesthetic formalism', a term that Teo applies to *PTU* and two other To films. Another issue that will be addressed in this book relates to the designation of To's oeuvre as 'action' films and of To himself as a specifically 'action' director, which I find at the very least questionable, and as I shall argue, again in the final chapter, misleading with reference to *PTU*. It seems as inapposite as calling

Scorsese, Kurosawa or Coppola 'action' directors, in spite of the gripping scenes of action integral to their films. Teo's rationale for his subtitle '*Director in Action*' is perhaps understandable in the Hong Kong context. However, Paul Willemen, among others, has already called into question the designation, explaining how it originated as a label of convenience in video stores, rather than as a specific critically and professionally acknowledged genre.[5] At the same time we recognise a contemporary type of 'action' film that is often culturally hybrid, if superficial in content. Self-consciously and formulaically global, this type of film aims at an intellectually undemanding viewer and is calculated to generate fast returns at the box office. Most of To's movies would be utterly misplaced in such a category. Action, as Willemen's article elucidates, is often loosely and lazily applied as a classification of films, frequently failing to encapsulate a screenwriter's script and director's mise-en-scène that is predicated, as To's best films are, on the relationship between action and inaction. Indeed, as we shall see, To's so-called action scenes revolve around gunplay as the predominant form of action, a convention which is more closely connected with western, *policier* and crime genres. I will argue, therefore that the genre of 'action' is a misnomer for To's body of work, and one that ultimately does not enhance appreciation of his personal style of filmmaking. In so doing I shall focus on his expertise in narrative development and his virtuosic use of film language.

The present study will concentrate on a single work by Johnnie To, namely *PTU*, and seek to explain the significance of what I propose as an underestimated gem of a film, indeed something of an unsung masterpiece, which the critical success of the major diptych *Election* and the recent European vogue for *Exiled* have caused to be overshadowed. The film's release was, as we shall see, unfortunate in its timing, at least from a commercial perspective. As regards the organisation of this book, it is intended to offer insights to those who know To's work, as well as to those who have only heard of his importance on the Hong Kong film scene. This opening chapter introduces the reader to his work and style. The succeeding one will focus on the issue of location and film space, the third will analyse the film's narrative in detailed sharp focus, and the final chapter will explore its allegorical signifying systems and aesthetic qualities, in addition to offering a critical assessment of the film's continuing topicality.

In assessing this work I hope to challenge a certain critical fallacy that seems to have taken root among critics and To admirers alike that *PTU* suffers from underdeveloped screenplay and characterisation. At the same time my wish is to enhance enjoyment, and dare I say, appreciation and understanding of the film's technical and thematic qualities, which are characteristically understated, subtle and artistically satisfying. It would have been rewarding to consider other examples of To's oeuvre, such as *The Mission*, *Election*, *Running Out of Time* (Teo's choice for To's best movie) or even *Exiled* for the distinction of a special study, the last-named being the Hong Kong selection for the 2008 Academy Awards. In some respects there would be more to say about some of these films from the point of view of character motivation and psychological complexity. However, *PTU* offers the viewer a more aesthetically rigorous and, I would argue, a more original film experience than these others, in spite of their many exceptional qualities. I believe that in years to come it will be seen as an example of a film director with a very personal signature style at the peak of his creative powers.

Film *cognoscenti* in a number of European countries including France, Germany and Italy (all with distinguished film traditions of their own) have noted To's development as a filmmaker of style and originality. In addition to sweeping the 2004 Golden Bauhinia awards in Hong Kong, *PTU* garnered a Prix du Jury award in 2004 at France's Festival de Cognac and both *Exiled* and *PTU* have been released to critical commendation recently in the U.K.

Yet in Hong Kong it is broadly true to say that this experienced director has been somewhat taken for granted. His fusion of highly aesthetically refined art-house cinematography and mise-en-scène with minimalist narrative exposition and development in established police and triad thriller and martial arts genres has perhaps contributed to this neglect. Hong Kong audiences appear to have assumed that he is a competent, if idiosyncratic, filmmaker of genre movies and to have focused mainly on his minimalist plots and taciturn characters without fully appreciating his stylised and often brilliantly realised film aesthetic. In part this misconception is due, as Teo has noted, to Johnnie To's work ethic and commitment to developing cinema in Hong Kong on a range of fronts. In part too, it is a result of Hong Kong commercial cinema's emphasis on star actors, who are vigorously marketed as though they were brand names, usually to the detriment of the creative and direction team behind this most collaborative of art forms. To has earned the reputation of being uncompromising in his demands and expectations on set, hardly the sort of attitude that endears him to the pampered young stars of Hong Kong cinema. A good example of this is his intolerance toward the use of private mobile phones on set, irrespective of the celebrity status of the user. One might say that the Hong Kong celebrity scene tends to admire him from a safe distance, while many local people seem to know that he is an important artist in Hong Kong but are not exactly sure why.

To started off directing and producing within the highly structured discipline of typical Hong Kong fast-output studio cinema, working on vehicles for emergent comedy star (now internationally established) Stephen Chow and other popular actors. Films like *Justice, My Foot* (1992) and *The Mad Monk* (1993) or *The Eighth Happiness* (1988, with Chow Yun Fat) were never going to win serious critical plaudits, quite apart from their screenplay and characterisation limitations, because comedy is less exportable, particularly the highly localised and often throw-away Hong Kong variety. *The Heroic Trio* (1993) and its sequel *Executioners* (1993), which To co-directed with respected action director Ching Siu-tung, became cult classics in the global video market. Indeed, To has spoken of his excellent working rapport and division of labour with Ching.[6] At this stage of his career To had his feet very firmly on the ground and recognised the need to balance the budget and avoid losing money on the films, with a main goal of making a modest profit for his investors. Subsequently he felt that his abilities would best be served by starting his own film production company, which was dubbed Milkyway Image at its inception in 1996. At this point of his career To began to concentrate on film production and brought in a stable of young directors like Patrick Yau and Patrick Leung and scriptwriting specialist Yau Nai-hoi as well as his colleague and friend Wai Ka-fai, with whom he has co-directed on a number of films (*Needing You*; *My Left Eye Sees Ghosts*; *Turn Left, Turn Right*; *Fulltime Killer*; *Running on Karma; The Mad Detective*). Nevertheless, his hand remains firmly on the tiller of the company, even though many of the co-directed and co-produced films are less impressive than his solo work as director.

In spite of his growing aspiration for wider regional and national recognition, as evidenced by the partly English-language and partly Japanese-language *Fulltime Killer* (2001), To continues to produce, and direct or co-direct, a dazzling array of films for Milkyway in a range of heterogeneous genres. Although his real *métier* in cinema appears to be the serious police-gangster film, he continues to direct and produce pot-boiler romantic comedies and zany comedies, so beloved of the Hong Kong public especially at Chinese New Year. Hence *Fat Choi Spirit* (2002) and *Yesterday Once More* (2004) accentuate the egregious nature of his approach to filmmaking. As a director who commands wide respect, To seems unconcerned about the stylistic variety and heterogeneity of his back catalogue. It is clear that he has always had an eye for commercial viability, having served his apprenticeship in television dramas and studio work in the 1980s and early 90s. Another factor to bear in mind is that To has been mindful of the sharp commercial decline in Hong Kong cinema since the Asian economic crisis of the late 1990s, a trend that is currently proving difficult to counteract, notwithstanding the city's strong economic revival.

One way of seeing his contribution to Hong Kong cinema of the last decade is that, very much as his 1997 fire-fighting movie *Lifeline* suggests, the heroism and team spirit of ordinary people are needed to get the city through the doldrums. To is clearly committed to Hong Kong cinema as an institution. Solid achievements, rather than bravura showmanship, are required in the current difficulties, hence the alternation between safe commercially viable cinema and what he may have regarded, especially when Milkyway was founded, as more self-indulgent, 'experimental', auteur-type projects. 'Exercises' are how he refers to such films in his fascinating interview with Teo.[7] In another interview with Shirley Lau for the *South China Morning Post*, To has clarified his compromise strategy of filmmaking: 'For every few commercial films I make, I have to do something that is entirely personal without considering what the market wants. There's a lot of satisfaction as well as pressure in it. But it's a regular exercise I use to evaluate myself.'[8]

In general one can say that To has succeeded in steering what in retrospect seems to be a judicious course between journeyman filmmaking of more conventional gangster, heroic drama and whimsical comedy genre movies in his earlier career and, latterly, increasingly idiosyncratic auteur-type projects. Nevertheless he continues to concentrate on screen action, or at least the filmic relationship between action and inaction, in many of his highly acclaimed films of recent years. *PTU* exemplifies this stylistic development, and for some commentators this and other recent To films may epitomise his emergence as an auteur director. However, as the Coen brothers have observed *apropos* of themselves, a collaborative, ensemble-oriented ethos of filmmaking rather tends to go against the grain of auteurship.[9] To's comedies and several of the co-directed films with Wai Ka-fai evince a tendency toward formulaic Hong Kong wackiness, carefree improbability or inconsistency and comic-book levity. Significantly, he reserves his own directorial credit for his most original and socially relevant work, which succeeds in shaping the *policier* and crime genres, rather in the great Hitchcock, Kurosawa and Melville tradition, to his own ends. We shall examine this connection more fully in chapters 3 and 4, especially with reference to Melville's fatalistic gangster-cop movies *Le Doulos* (1963), *Le Cercle Rouge* (1970) (of which it may be observed that the Buddhist scriptural quotation of the opening appears to have inspired the opening reference of Hong Kong's own *Infernal Affairs*), and *Un Flic* (*Dirty Money*, 1972). However, it is significant that Melville's great lead actor Alain Delon is deliberately referenced in *Fulltime Killer* — Andy Lau's professional killer informing a lesser species of thug that he should see a certain, unspecified French film (presumably *Le Samouraï*, 1967) to understand that you do not mess with an ice-cool professional hit man. Of course To is not alone among Hong Kong film directors in his evident admiration for the work of both Kurosawa and Melville.

To's approach to direction, particularly in the cooperatively creative context of his Milkyway Images production house, flies in the face of received wisdom about commercial filmmaking. His casting preference for character types and his reliance on a core of ensemble actors stand in sharp contrast to Hong Kong's Hollywood-esque star system. Granted his ensembles include household Hong Kong names such as Anthony Wong, Andy Lau, Cecilia Cheung and Louis Koo, as well as professionally admired actors of the calibre of Simon Yam, Lau Ching-wan, Ruby Wong, Lam Suet, Nick Cheung and Francis Ng. However the film is never a vehicle for the star name in a Johnnie To work; rather the actor must sublimate his or her ego to the requirements of the director's cinematic flair and sensibility. Perhaps To's scepticism about conventional Hong Kong–style heroism in his more recent films and his tendency to eschew the romantic stereotypes of Tsui Hark and John Woo in favour of more mundane and yet more psychologically compelling protagonists have disappointed those in Hong Kong who like their cinema to be predictable, generic and Hollywood-heroic. And yet, To remains addicted to action and crime genres, albeit adapted to his own narrative and ideological purposes. It is precisely this quality of ambivalence in To's films and in the way he playfully subverts and yet respects crime and action genres, I believe, that makes his recent films special, much in the same way that Coen brothers' films are special to the initiated. The analogy is far from gratuitous since there are a number of similarities in their respective approaches to filmmaking, including idiosyncratic perspectives on life, as well as a distinct predilection for ensemble work and for using a small group of core actors supplemented by the occasional star name in most of his movies. Clearly, the Coens' use of Frances McDormand, Steve Buscemi, John Turturro and others on a regular basis can be seen as a distinctive element of their signature style of filmmaking.

Significantly, the *PTU* acting ensemble has been retained for what can be seen as a series of sequels or spin-offs being produced for television based on To's original idea for his 2003 film. These four tele-films plus one feature film have already been shot and are in post-production at present (November 2008). The same actors as the source film appear in freshly generated storylines with altered names, an attempt perhaps to demarcate a clear distance between them and the earlier film. The first of the four, entitled *Tactical Unit — The Code*, has already been shown in festivals, including the October 2008 Hong Kong Asian Film Festival. It was directed by *PTU* editor and associate director Law Wing-cheong with To at the production helm again, as in *Eye in the Sky*. Picking up some of the themes of *PTU*, this film focuses on an investigation by the Complaints Against the Police body (CAPO) in response to allegations of brutality against a triad suspect by members of the PTU unit. According to initial critical reaction, this first in the series of planned sequels has much in common with *PTU* without managing to capture the moody suspense and cinematic flair of what in adaptation terminology may be called its 'parent' text. At the time of writing the latest spin-off is *Tactical Unit — Comrade in Arms* (December 2008). Clearly, the decision to spawn sequels from *PTU* by the Milkyway team seems to reflect a renewed interest in the film in Hong Kong and wider appreciation of its quirky originality than seemed likely back in 2003.

PTU and the SARS year: Hong Kong's longest night

The rationale for this case study of *PTU* is that the film is the most distinctive in the To back catalogue, the one that is hardest to place or categorise and the one that demands most engagement, or at least concentration, from the spectator. The tense, moody ambience of films such as *The Mission*, and more recently *Exiled*, and the obsessive and pathological character study of the two *Election* films (in many respects To's *Godfather*, if I can be forgiven the analogy) rightly make these films stand out as major works of the last ten years. None of these films, however, explores the group-individual dichotomy quite as compellingly, grittily and economically as *PTU*, for all their undoubted stylishness. No other To film challenges our idea of cinema as effectively as this one or generates quite such *jouissance* (pleasure) of the transgressive text, to use Barthes's term. Like some other To works, the film has fallen between the cracks of art-house and commercial categorization. *PTU* was several years in the making, which is generally anathema in Hong Kong terms and something of a milestone in To's film output. Just as *Election* can — and indeed has been — considered as a socially allegorical work, with the ongoing debate about Hong Kong's political system and the city's political dependence on China as its point of reference, so too is it possible to see in *PTU* much more than a police-triad genre vehicle, but rather a socio-political 'essay' on police powers and practices, public safety and deadly virus-like incursions from across the border. Indeed, some Chinese-language commentators took the allegory further, going so far as to liken the bumbling central character in the film to Hong Kong's hapless chief executive at the time, Tung Chee-hwa. Such speculative insights are, in my view, best filed under 'interesting', but they are not particularly helpful in approaching the film's main concerns.

There is no doubt, however, that *PTU* can be justifiably interpreted as allegorical and emblematic of post-millennial events in Hong Kong. During a time of great uncertainty about Hong Kong's future, and indeed its present, the 2003 film reflected the ambivalent mood of the city perfectly. The film's release coincided with the SARS outbreak and the socio-economic trough that Hong Kong was experiencing in that most difficult year. SARS — severe acute respiratory syndrome, to give the disease its full name — seemed at the time to be an epidemic of potentially catastrophic proportions, almost a Black Death of the twenty-first century. As it transpired, the outbreak was contained thanks to the brave and unremitting efforts of the medical profession, and in the vast majority of cases the virus was isolated and successfully treated. In the spring of 2003, however, people were afraid to go out for fear of contracting the disease, and the usually bustling Hong Kong streets were uncharacteristically empty. At night the streets assumed an even eerier quality which the film conveys, more unintentionally than intentionally, since To had started work on it in 2000 and deferred completion while he worked on other more commercial projects. *PTU*'s darkness, both literal and metaphorical, and its distinctly film noir ambience evoked the sombre mood of Hong Kong people in much the same way that Andrew Lau and Alan Mak's *Infernal Affairs* trilogy of the same period did. By contrast with the latter films, however, To's work had a quirky, ironic humour that defied total pessimism.

In its representation of *esprit de corps* and collective trust, at least at street level, To's film conveyed, perhaps in its guardedly optimistic outcome, a sense of light at the end of Hong Kong's dark night that had started in 1998 with the Asian economic downturn. In more pragmatic terms, though, the timing of the film's release was far from perfect. The box-office take — just under HK$3 million — was predictably disappointing, given the painstaking work that had gone into the making of the film. On the other hand, considering the prevailing mood of Hong Kong in the spring of 2003 and the dearth of humans outside their flats and offices, *PTU* performed creditably, and has gone on to justify the time, money and effort expended by all associated with it. Moreover, as To pointed out in interview, the box-office revenue for *PTU* was approximately the same as that for *The Mission*, a film one would have expected to be considerably more popular on account of its subject matter. The latter film was released in more advantageous, non-SARS circumstances, although the Asian economic crisis had already made its impact felt in the film industry by the turn of the millennium. In many ways a watershed film for To, *The Mission*'s laconic style and pattern of alternation between inertia and rapid action laid the foundations for his film method of the new millennium and his emergence both as a filmmaker of note outside Hong Kong and as, arguably, the most significant contemporary Hong Kong filmmaker in the context of Hong Kong itself.

As *South China Morning Post* critic Paul Fonoroff observed in his uncharacteristically complimentary review after the film went on general release in May 2003, *PTU* shows To at his most mature as a filmmaker: 'Lean and sparse, with a pleasant sprinkling of dark humour and an absence of maudlin sentimentality, *PTU* is one of To's most mature works and the most satisfying local production so far this year [2003] ... Those willing to don face masks will find there is still life in a film industry whose demise has long been predicted, but which like Inspector Lo [one of the protagonists, an OCTB (Organised Crime and Triad Bureau) sergeant, not an inspector] somehow manages to see a new dawn.'[10] A more distanced and non-local perspective on the film is offered by *Time Out*'s cryptically semi-anonymous reviewer (TJ) after the film's 2007 release in the U.K. The reviewer commented that 'the director's unruffled poise and the striking nocturnal camera work are a source of pleasure in themselves',[11] but opined that the script was 'not fully formed' (an ironically unintentional understatement, given that the script was largely improvised). TJ concludes with the verdict that 'the murder investigation and the missing firearm provide just enough plot to get the movie through the night, even though the character relationships are on the sketchy side'.[12]

Still 1 Sgt Lo with bandaged head.

The film's Hong Kong première had actually taken place in the context of the 27th Hong Kong International Film Festival's gala opening section a month prior to its Hong Kong general circuit release. The International Film Festival (HKIFF) has long been a major cultural event for the would-be 'world city', placing New Hong Kong Cinema side-by-side with other examples of world cinema in the public view. This practice is generally good for the image and the development of Hong Kong cinema, since its other award and recognition mechanisms have the tendency to be parochial and somewhat self-congratulatory. The Film Festival as a Hong Kong institution is not without its own controversies, especially in respect of its choice of films and challenges to notions of its objectivity and autonomy. However it offers, in general, a critical, international yardstick by which Hong Kong films can be judged as well as a forum for evaluating Hong Kong cinema of the past in retrospective terms as a body of work in the cultural history of the city. In other words, the critical frame afforded any Hong Kong film by inclusion in the Festival emphasises its qualities as a cultural and aesthetic artefact, as opposed to an entertainment commodity — the latter approximating more closely to the image that an understandably consumerist-oriented local industry is apt to promote.

Given prime place at the Hong Kong Cultural Centre's Grand Theatre together with Yamada Yoji's *The Twilight Samurai*, the film was certainly showcased as the best of current Hong Kong cinema. In the HKIFF's programme of screenings, *PTU*'s plot is playfully, if slightly irritatingly, summarised in punning reference to To's impressive back catalogue:

> Set against a Tsimshatsui that never sleeps, among sultry neon lights and thousand shades of electric blue, a stolen police gun triggers a suspenseful chain of events that click into place like a Rubic's cube. Sir Sa, a fallen cop [*sic*] who just swaggered out of *The Bad Lieutenant*, endures The Longest Nite in his life. First his car gets vandalised, then his butt gets kicked. Suddenly he's wedged between two gangs on the brink of a bloodbath, while staving off investigations by both the Anti-Vice Squad [Organised Crime and Triad Bureau] and Homicide Unit [Criminal Investigation Department] embroiled in their own turf war. His only Lifeline is a maverick team of 'blue berets' (the titular Police Tactical Unit) which tries to recover his gun by hook or by crook. With all parties armed to the hilt converging at 4 p.m. [*sic* – it should be 4 a.m.]

he's Running Out of Time. A Hero Never Dies, but in Johnnie To's cynical world, the heroes are the bad guys, so up till the last frame, Expect the Unexpected![13]

Still 2 Tsim Sha Tsui — a district that never sleeps.

The above preview's reference to the 1998 film *The Longest Nite*, produced by To but directed by Patrick Yau with To's collaboration, is particularly germane to any discussion of *PTU*. Like *PTU*, the action of *The Longest Nite* is determined to a considerable extent by the temporal compression of the events — a rogue cop involved in a cat-and-mouse game with a professional hit man, who is in many respects his double — but the compression of time and plot in the later film is even more acute. Indeed one can always find echoes and thematic repetitions across To's body of work as a whole, so that to an extent we can consider To's approach to his films as a series of themes and variations played out from one picture to another. In *The Longest Nite* the action takes place in Macau over a period of twenty-four hours. The other similarity between the two movies is the portrayal of the cop whose strategies are based on the amoral belief in the ends justifying the means. As Teo has elucidated in his study of To's work, the *jianghu* (roughly translated as loyalty, brotherhood, etc.) themes which are woven into the very fabric of modern Hong Kong filmmaking have influenced To's creative ideas, as have the *doppelgänger* motif of cop and robber as mirror images of each other (very much an important motif in *The Longest Nite*). Graphic violence and a deterministic, inexorable end-game are also very much ingredients of this earlier film. Whilst *PTU* presents a far more complex and ambivalent scenario regarding the use of violence necessitated by motives of self-preservation, it is clear that To's cinema is part of a discourse on violence and power, on professionalism and ethical responsibility in Hong Kong society. This is a post-1997 discourse shared by such films as the *Infernal Affairs* trilogy, but not by pre-1997 anxiety films, whose moral universe was significantly different.

In this connection, one of the purposes of the present study is to explore how To, especially in *PTU*, deconstructs the genre and character types of the established 'heroic bloodshed' Hong Kong tradition dating back to the 1980s and to John Woo's *A Better Tomorrow* and Ringo Lam's *City on Fire* in particular. This is not to say that To is free of the formative influence of the representations offered by that ground-breaking sub-genre. The 1980s phenomenon coincided with To's gradual emergence as a fledgling filmmaker following his early TVB career, and it was natural for his development to be marked by such an important indigenous cinematic movement. However, the 'heroic bloodshed' genre, for all the excitement and originality it exuded, relied heavily on elements of Western cinema, including the graphic violence of Sam Peckinpah, and also on other Asian genres, such as the *wuxia* or martial arts film. Indeed, referring to the models for his characters in *A Better Tomorrow*, Woo cited a litany of Hollywood and French New Wave movie stars (especially the ultimately cool Alain Delon) as his idols.[14] Whether or not To sets out deliberately to dismantle this construction of the heroic idol, which has so much dominated Hong Kong popular culture, is open to debate, and my fourth and final chapter will discuss this question in greater depth. His preference for deconstructive, ironic comedy and for semi-heroic or anti-heroic depictions certainly challenges the 'serious' conventions of the action film and the police thriller genres. Whilst this is not a consistent facet of To's filmmaking, such anti-heroic representation is integral to the highly acclaimed triad films, *Election I* and *II*. The major difference between the *Election* diptych and *PTU* is the former's skilful integration of character study with narrative by contrast with the earlier film's subordination of character to plot/action.

Moreover, like Woo's *A Better Tomorrow* and Jackie Chan's original *Police Story* (1985), *PTU* is quintessentially Hong Kong in subject matter. Perhaps more than either of these earlier films, it conveys the sense of a genuine Hong Kong locale to such an extent that one might even claim that Tsim Sha Tsui, where the film is set, is in a way the subject (or even the hero!) of the film. As we will see in the following chapter, To's skilfully constructed depiction of Tsim Sha Tsui succeeds in capturing a spirit of place that is more convincing than the superficial sense of locale suggested by many run-of-the-mill Hong Kong films. One of the most evocative screen portraits of the streets of Tsim Sha Tsui, especially those to the north between Nathan Road and Chatham Road, the film shows another side of Tsim Sha Tsui, during the early hours of the morning when only police patrols and potential criminals are on the streets. There are some almost surreal shots of shops and streets — in particular Tom Lee Music in Cameron Lane — eerily empty, unfamiliar and threatening. Another very recent Milkyway film, *Eye in the Sky* (2007), on which To is credited for duties on the production side, but in whose direction he was also involved creatively, offers a similarly atmospheric, well-crafted depiction of locale, but this time mainly set around Hong Kong–side's Central District.

Still 3 Tom Lee shot.

The basic narrative of *PTU* is simple, although wickedly ironic, and appears superficially similar to the central idea of mainland director Lu Chuan's 2002 thriller *The Missing Gun*. The latter might have subconsciously influenced the firearm plot device, even though work on To's film was begun prior to the release of Lu's. However, in an interview for Jean-Pierre Le Dionnet's *Des Films* release of *PTU* in France, To denied ever having seen *The Missing Gun* and was emphatic about the gestation of *PTU*'s plot and themes in his own experience, observation and imagination. The film's compression of narrative time into a single night may call to mind for cinema buffs two American movies — Martin Scorsese's *After Hours* and John Carpenter's *The Assault on Precinct 13* — but these works, whilst enjoyable and well-made films in their own right, have only a very superficial resemblance to To's plot. A closer parallel with To's creative scenario might be Akira Kurosawa's 1949 noir *policier*, *Stray Dog*, set in Tokyo, in which Kurosawa's main man, Toshiro Mifune, plays a rookie detective whose gun has been stolen. *The Missing Gun* may or may not have been inspired by Kurosawa's tense tale, but such is the film industry's predilection for borrowing and remaking that it is hardly unreasonable to discern a connection. To's admiration for Kurosawa is well documented, but the influence of Melville, and especially *Le Cercle Rouge*, which the French director claims as a deliberate experiment in evoking the shadowy quality of noir, but paradoxically in colour — exactly what To does in *PTU* — is perhaps less well appreciated.

Topicality, theatricality and film noir

PTU's wonderfully symmetrical but apparently dislocated narrative focuses on a concatenation of minor events starting with the loss of Anti-Crime Squad Sergeant Lo Sa's gun in a scrap with local punks, a misfortune that looks to cost him his forthcoming promotion. Lo's consternation over disciplinary procedure and the certain loss of promotion is mitigated by the commitment of PTU officer Sergeant Mike Ho to help him find the gun before dawn in the course of his Unit's (Police Tactical Unit, hence the film's title) nocturnal patrol. In one scene the chubby Lo, played with great aplomb by To regular Lam Suet, is greeted by the mountainous triad uncle Chung, played with equal zest by veteran film director Wong Tin-lam, as 'Fei jai' (fat boy) in typically direct and politically incorrect Hong Kong style. This gloriously ironic case of the pot calling the kettle black epitomises To's trademark earthy, streetwise, deadpan Hong Kong wit, and highlights his skilful use of an ensemble of 'character actors', eschewing the pretty-boy film star/pop-singer star turns conventionally employed in most commercial vehicles of Hong Kong cinema. One of the visual metaphors of the opening sequence of the film presents an incongruous symmetry between police officer (Lo), triad gang (Ponytail and his bullies), and young nervous-looking customer in the hot-pot restaurant. A dripping air-conditioner sets in train the sequence of initially innocuous incidents on which the plot hinges. As the triangular power struggle is presented wryly and with critical distance, we see that Lo's tactics are similar to those of Ponytail and his gang. The weakest of the visual trio, the one who has to keep shifting tables, ironically and unexpectedly has the last word, or rather deed, in this scene. His sudden brazen knife murder of Ponytail is of central significance as the starting point for a series of events in which he superficially plays no further part.

Still 4 Mike Ho (Simon Yam).

The tense, skilfully plotted and atmospherically shot movie uses locations near the Tsim Sha Tsui commercial areas, as well as other diverse Hong Kong and Kowloon locations intended to be seen as contiguous to the streets depicted in the movie's establishing shots, remarkably effectively and imaginatively. Whilst the narrative appears circumstantial and fragmented, there is at the same time a sense of fateful, ironic significance in the detail that is only evident to the viewer in the film's explosive but ironically distanced dénouement. In a whirlwind climax involving triad gangsters, Mike, played by the popular Hong Kong actor Simon Yam, and 'Fei Lo' are inadvertently caught up in a deadly but farcically coincidental end-game. Lo discovers his gun just in time, in every sense of the word. The dark atmosphere, laconic wit and unflinching depiction of the seamy side of the city and of certain police practices make this a movie to appreciate only after you have experienced the streets of TST — as it is called in its pragmatically compressed local acronym — in full daytime and evening swing.

As French playwright Jean Anouilh put it, comparing dramatic action to a well-oiled machine, in his modern version of Sophocles' tragedy, *Antigone*, 'the spring of dramatic inevitability is coiled and ready for action ... One has only to watch and let things happen'.[15] What unfolds in the chain of circumstances that follows, linking the missing gun to the random slaying of the son of a triad boss and to both local and mainland criminals, appears to us as at first delightfully aleatory and at a later point of the film ironically inevitable. Whether we label it as circumstance or 'happenstance', rarely has the well-sprung coil of tragic inevitability of the theatrical mode been employed to such devastating effect in cinema. Indeed the ironically fatalistic spirit of Anouilh's adaptation of *Antigone* is echoed by To's equally whimsical but fatalistic approach to an oft-told tale. The ending of the movie could just as well be tragic, although as fate and the screenwriters would have it, it is only tragic for the gangsters. Like the *Infernal Affairs* trilogy, *PTU*'s narrative blurred the boundary between police and triads, and underneath its conventional 'good guys/bad guys' surface suggested that methods of operating and extracting information on the mean streets were not entirely dissimilar. Melville's Parisian police and thieves in *Un Flic* and *Le Cercle Rouge* are similarly indistinct from one another in a number of disturbing particulars. The mean streets in question in *PTU* are those of Kowloon's main commercial district, Tsim Sha Tsui, focus of the entertainment industry and therefore of the triad gangs and protection rackets. It is not for nothing that Teo refers to the film as a kind of 'Kowloon noir'.[16] In To's film the area is seen, literally and metaphorically, in an unusual light. Indeed, Tsim Sha Tsui as a nocturnal setting is foregrounded in the film to the extent that it almost dominates the characters depicted in To's wittily circumstantial tale. The back streets of Tsim Sha Tsui close to Nathan Road are depicted in To's cinematic vision as a murky underworld where danger lurks around each corner.

Still 5 In the alley (bluish light).

This transformation of a familiar bustling district that is very much the pulse of Hong Kong's commercial life into a defamiliarised and ambivalent milieu is achieved through evocative use of lighting, cinematography and mise-en-scène. The few locations chosen for the setting of To's film are skilfully transformed into quasi-stage settings. Indeed the film achieves a theatrical concentration of setting, character and action akin to the so-called theatrical unities that distinguishes it from the typical episodic, spatially and temporally dispersed film narrative. To has referred in interview (see Appendix) to the theatre-like distance between spectator and characters through the use of wide shots and also to the theatre-like structure of the conceptual scene arrangement. In his view there are seven main scenes in the film and in chapter 3 I delineate the film's seven contiguous plot strands, which are theatrically interlinked in a way that is very unusual for contemporary cinema. One of the most theatrical elements of the film overall is To's deliberate focus on the centre of the mise-en-scène, which blurs the periphery of the frame, rather in the way that a theatre composition tends to de-emphasise the margins of the stage leading to the wings. Another is his use of setting as a constant dynamic with characters arriving and departing, as they would on a stage. This is particularly true of the setting of the dénouement (in itself a very theatrical term denoting untying the knots, in other words, resolution). In the final scene it is the street itself — the locus of action — that remains a constant presence, more so than the actors who come and go. In this process of what may be described as 'theatricalisation', the film constructs an imaginary, almost hypothetical Tsim Tsa Tsui, one where familiar places in streets like Cameron Road become unfamiliar, when To slyly interpolates a non-existent alley way, for example. The music shop (Tom Lee Music) in Cameron Lane (abutting Cameron Road) really exists, but the alley where the police unit beat up an asthmatic informer and petty criminal until he requires artificial resuscitation is a Hong Kong–side transplant. Because the continuity and the seamless editing of the film suggest that the alley is really there, one is shocked to find that it has somehow 'disappeared' in real life. It is as if some Narnia-like revelation will open the alley up and we can step into it, as the children step through the wardrobe into a parallel reality in the C. S. Lewis tale. The same thing happens in the final shoot-out scene, which is supposed to be set in Canton Road in Kowloon, but was actually filmed in Lee King Road, Ap Lei Chau, on the south side of Hong Kong Island. We convince ourselves we recognise the transplanted location as an authentic setting. But nothing in the film is exactly what it seems.

Furthermore, the film's topicality is remarkable. In addition to its evocation of the downbeat mood of the SARS year, the missing police officer's gun, which plays such a central, if inanimate role, is highly topical. In 2001 the mysterious murder in an apparently innocuous housing estate incident of Constable Leung Shin-yan and the theft of his police-issue revolver was an unsolved crime. Subsequently the perpetrator, a fellow policeman named Tsui Po-ko, died in a shoot-out with two patrolling constables in Tsim Sha Tsui in April 2006. There were rumours of a police cover-up, but no clear picture emerged in the media, except the fact that Tsui was a rogue officer with a megalomaniac personality, a scenario that is uncannily represented in the film *Infernal Affairs* by the Andy Lau character, or indeed even earlier by Tony Leung's portrayal of the venal, anti-hero Sam in Yau and To's *The Longest Nite*. The real-life mystery surrounding the use of the dead constable's firearm — for the Hong Kong police a missing police-issue weapon is of extremely serious consequence — also inevitably brought to mind the *PTU* plot device. Does life imitate the art of Hong Kong film directors' cinematic imagination? To's seeming prescience and topicality about real-life, socially relevant issues were evident much earlier in his 1997 fire brigade movie *Lifeline*, which also explored the theme of *esprit de corps*. The film was released just a month after the Garley Building fire in Jordan, Hong Kong's most deadly blaze in recent memory.

Global/local: Johnnie To, Hong Kong cinema and the international context

It is possible to read a political subtext into *PTU* that is very critical of the apparent gang-like nature of the police, since this is what is implied by the incompatibility of the positive, semi-heroic representation at the beginning of the film and the less flattering portrait that follows. Yet To denies us a simplistic vision of his subjects. For him, police and criminals are complementary groups often operating in the shadows of society. In his follow-up film to *PTU*, *Breaking News*, the media representation of a policeman who pleads (successfully) for his life with a gun-wielding criminal is implicitly more critical of media stereotypes than it is of police inadequacy. In short, To's films humanise (as Wong Kar-wai's do too) a Hong Kong that has been increasingly mythologised and dehumanised by formulaic genre films among other types of media. The ambivalent moral universe of the film tends to connote the random, arbitrary nature of life in general and police-triad relations in particular. To's uncompromising challenge to comfortable filmic preconceptions of 'good violence' and 'bad violence' leaves the audience with more social and moral questions than answers. As a filmmaker he is at his best when analysing and questioning *idées reçues* (received ideas), such as that of loyalty and comradeship among police officers and among gangsters. The choices and decisions made by his characters reveal the relative and circumstantial nature of such interactions, and portray the strains placed upon the individual by the demands of collective norms of behaviour. Fate, luck, serendipity — all play their part in disentangling the threads of narrative complication and reuniting the errant gun with its perplexed but tenacious owner. At one point Lo pleads comically with the vengeful gang boss, 'Baldhead': 'I'm out of my depth. I just want to get my gun back.' The film's Western-style 'showdown' at the end has something in common with other action films that depict sudden explosive violence after a slow, tense build-up to the narrative climax. And yet its slow-motion aesthetic epitomises To's auteurish instincts, where stillness, not movement, is at the heart of the composition.

David Bordwell, who has described *PTU* as 'an oblique, off-centre thriller with a unique flavour', includes To in his list of Hong Kong directors who have adopted what Bordwell sees as a contemporary cinematographic style of 'intensified continuity'.[17] According to Bordwell, this phenomenon of popular cinema represented an attempt to engage the viewer with greater immediacy than ever before in the medium. Average shot lengths were reduced over three decades from five to eight seconds to as little as two to three seconds. The ratio of tight close-ups and medium close-ups to establishing shots and medium-long shots also increased dramatically, and 'sliding or arcing or circling or swooping' tracking shots were designed to make camera movement more imitative of rapid motion. In Bordwell's view, the technological innovations of the 1980s, particularly lightweight camera systems and the home video, contributed to this dramatic evolution in the modern cinema's kinesic aesthetics. In the same article Bordwell goes on to compare the increasingly accelerated cutting rates and tighter close-up ratio of Hollywood and Hong Kong films from the 1980s onwards in order to promote excitement in the viewer. He asserts that the sense of rhythm of Hong Kong filmmakers, 'steeped in a tradition of expressive movement', enables them to adapt the stylistic strategies of the intensified continuity movement particularly effectively. In general, however, too rigid an application of this stylistic term to To, and particularly to *PTU*, would be problematic, since To's solo work is often more restrained than other Hong Kong directors. It also tends to be kinesically character-driven rather than action-driven. His preference for unusual mise-en-scène detail, as well as medium perspective composition over tight facial close-ups — of which there are comparatively few in *PTU* — and slow atmospheric build-up, contrasts strongly with the more flamboyant, adrenalin-pumping cinematography of action directors like John Woo.

Nevertheless, Bordwell's definition of what he calls 'the prowling camera' to facilitate 'versatile tracking shots' is particularly applicable to a number of scenes in *PTU*, especially the one where Mike's team are carrying out a stealthy and potentially dangerous raid on a factory building. This prowling camera scene culminates in complete anti-climax, since only a group of unarmed gang girlfriends are present. To's alternation between expressive rapid camera movement and his brilliantly evocative and suspenseful static shots, particularly in the cunningly postponed dénouement and showdown, in some ways confirms Bordwell's application of the theory to Hong Kong cinema and in others undercuts it. To's cinematic style stretches suspense and unpredictability to lengths that the Hong Kong cinema-going public, brought up on a diet of fast action and comedy films, can find intolerable. His average shot length in solo films does not conform to the fast-cutting theory of contemporary cinema. Especially not in *PTU*, in which long takes are at the centre of To's strategy of alternating tedium (albeit atmospheric tedium!) with suspenseful, but often anti-climactic false climaxes. It is no coincidence that an earlier To film (he was producer but again assisted director Patrick Yau in the creative process), also about the police, is entitled *Expect the Unexpected*. This 1998 work exudes, to quote Bordwell, an air of 'blunt, bleak nihilism'.[18] In *Expect the Unexpected* the police officers are gunned down at the end, in stark contrast to *PTU*'s felicitous outcome, but the tension created by uncertainty and unpredictability is for To an intrinsic element of both his story development and his philosophy of life in general. As he implies in many of his films, life plays many tricks on us, while imposing its random sequence of routine predictable hours, uneventful *longueurs* and occasional bursts of frenetic activity.

Still 6 Stairwell — Mike and torch.

To's collaborators Yau Nai-hoi and Au Kin-yee on the screenplay, Cheng Siu-keung on the cinematography, Stephen Ma and Jerome Fung on the artistic and visual effects and especially Chung Chi-wing on the atmospheric and ethereally chilly music score, make valuable contributions to the seamless quality of this compellingly tense film. The art of the film is understated yet stunningly effective in each of its components, with no cynical commercial ploy imposed by producers to sully its composition and creation. The reason for this virtue is that To's filmmaking has reached a stage of healthy financial and creative autonomy, allowing him to concentrate in this film, as in *The Mission*, *Election* and *Sparrow*, on the sort of film he really wants to make. He has clearly benefited from a stripped-down approach to narrative and characterisation, avoiding the melodramatic back-story elements employed in the otherwise enjoyable and well-made *Lifeline*. The baroque approach to subject matter and style remains evident in his collaborative films, *Running on Karma* (also 2003) being a good example. Wai Ka-fai's involvement in co-directed projects may enhance for some filmgoers the fantastical comic-book side of To's cinema persona, but there is little doubt that his absence on films such as *PTU*, *Election* and *Exiled* guarantees greater rigour and intensity. Without Wai Ka-fai we clearly see a more tight-knit approach to the plotting of the narrative and an avoidance of the extraneous and illogical elements that had come to characterise the off-beat style of much contemporary Hong Kong filmmaking.

Whether or not cinematic realism is also enhanced when To works solo is a matter of debate, since in their own way these films may appear to the non–Hong Kong viewer as stylised and idiosyncratic as films like *Fulltime Killer* and *Running on Karma*. From my own perspective, however, what I would describe as To's stylised realism is more grounded in a Hong Kong we know, as opposed to a parody based on American comic-book imports or much contemporary Hollywood 'eye-candy'. Moreover such cinema has the ring of authenticity and the feel of a master in action, and crucially, is tighter in construction and stronger in credibility than the more self-indulgently esoteric Wai Ka-fai influences, however popular they may be with the novelty-loving Hong Kong public. Stephen Teo is generous in his recognition of the value of collaborators in To's cinematic co-operative, but he rightly privileges To's personal cinematic vision as of paramount importance.

To's roots are as much in the Asian cinema of Hong Kong's genre films as they are in great directors like Hitchcock, Kurosawa, Peckinpah, Scorsese, Melville and, as Teo has fascinatingly suggested, in Japanese master Yasujiro Ozu.[19] His cinema is, however, for the time being, distinctively Hong Kong rather than transnational, although he has clearly absorbed the qualities of great cinema. Whether he is tempted by the lure of directing in the West remains to be seen. Ang Lee has done Hollywood on his own terms, and remained creative, much more so than John Woo, who has tended to stagnate in recent years. As for To, he enjoys considerable creative freedom within the context of Milkyway Image, and on virtually all of the company's film projects he exercises the right of quality control and production overview. His backers trust him with their investment, and he in turn accepts responsibility for box-office success (inevitably limited, as in the case of *PTU*, or pronounced in the case of *Election*) with the proviso that there is no artistic interference in the film on the part of the investors. This state of affairs would not obtain were he to accept a film project associated with the Hollywood system, as he acknowledges. He has received attractive offers to direct projects outside Hong Kong, but admits to being hesitant in case expressive-artistic restrictions are imposed upon his work. 'Film is a projection of one's own culture, and you need a field of creation,' he asserts. 'As a filmmaker, you have to realize what you can create and where you can best create it. Films you can make overseas must necessarily be different from what can be made in Hong Kong.'[20]

Bordwell, with characteristic perspicacity, has identified the problems associated with 'flying in' directors to make Hollywood projects more exotic-looking. A director needs time to develop a body of work and, as Bordwell points out in relation to Hong Kong cinema, 'rapid turnover, high-output cinema tends to provide not *low* quality but a *range* of quality. Most films will be negligible, and many will be just fair. Yet some will probably be good, and a few may be excellent. How can this happen?' I shall here propose *PTU* as a good example of Bordwell's thesis and one that illustrates excellence emerging from a steady output and an increasingly distinctive body of work. Flair must be allied to craftsmanship and a career dedicated to filmmaking. There are exceptions, of course, whereby first-time filmmakers produce a master-work, but, as in most trades, years of experience and learning the ropes are required before individual flair can be fully realised and high-quality work achieved. Perhaps the present study can help to answer Bordwell's rhetorical question.

If a more globalised project were to be considered, a French or European co-production might suit the creative side of To much better than Hollywood. The aesthetics of To's cinema have changed markedly from the period of his Hollywood influences, as, for example, when *Lifeline* was unhelpfully compared with *Backdraft*. When Andrew Lau and Alan Mak's admired *Infernal Affairs* trilogy metamorphosed into the Scorsese Oscar-winning vehicle *The Departed* in 2006, there was inevitable speculation surrounding other Hong Kong candidates for the Hollywood makeover. However, the likelihood of a *Departed*-style transplant whereby *PTU* is remade in New York or Los Angeles appears minimal. For one thing, there is not a lot of irony in Los Angeles, or at any event in Hollywood. For another, where would they find an actor as unselfishly and unconventionally charismatic as Lam Suet? Perhaps one way of looking at To's achievement in *PTU* is that his study of the Hong Kong police, warts and all, can be compared to the job of film directing. You never quite know what you are going to get, things do not always work out satisfactorily and there are lots of compromises in doing the job. But at the same time, there is a strong work ethic and sense of commitment and responsibility. At the end of the day you do the job according to the best of your ability and in spite of all the constraints, and hope to get home at least safely, even if in the small hours or right before the dawn! This seems to me to sum up Johnnie To's philosophy of work and filmmaking.[21]

2

'Into the Perilous Night' — Police and Gangsters in the Hong Kong Mean Streets

'It [the cinema] is not the same as the other arts, which aim rather at something unreal through the world, but makes the world itself something unreal or a tale. With the cinema, it is the world which becomes its own image, and not an image which becomes world.'
— Gilles Deleuze, *Cinema 1 — The Movement Image*, 59

'Even the dark, gloomy and ordinary places can be infiltrated with emotions, which, under the transformation of the camera, the imagination fuses with the real. You may still recognise these locations at a glance, but they are no longer the reality.'
— Lawrence Pun, *The Emotional Map of Hong Kong Cinema* in Hong Kong Film Archive, @LOCATION, 75

'To look at Hong Kong cinema within a spectrum of diverse representations of urban space, we find different efforts from one extreme of allegorical space to the other of realist space, and in between the search for identity in nostalgic, hyper-real and simulated space. In recent years directors have also tried to return

> to a sense of place with a renewed awareness of the relationship between cinema and the city, making particular references to the issue of cultural identity.'
>
> — Leung Ping-kwan, 'Urban Cinema and the Cultural Identity of Hong Kong' in *Between Home and World — A Reader in Hong Kong Cinema*, 394

Cinema and the city: Tsim Sha Tsui noir

Respected local critic, academic and creative writer Leung Ping-kwan has astutely identified the inter-space between accurate and realistic representations of a recognisable Hong Kong milieu and the Baudrillard-esque hyper-real spaces that are evoked in many Hong Kong films, including such classics as *Rouge*, *In the Mood for Love* and *Infernal Affairs*. Such simulated reality in the depiction of place is typical of a virtual reality culture and technology, and we should acknowledge the huge shift in the modern film industry where digital techniques can blur the boundaries between fantastical and putatively realistic narrative genres. That said, famous pre-digital age Hong Kong films, such as *The World of Suzie Wong* and *Love Is a Many-Splendoured Thing*, brazenly and cheerfully misrepresented specific Hong Kong places, unambiguously referred to in the source novels, in their choice of shooting location. All in all, experience tells us not to believe the evidence of our eyes when we watch any Hong Kong film set in Hong Kong. Jackie Chan's *Police Story IV* would have us believe that the young criminals can abseil down buildings in Tsim Sha Tsui and land on terra firma in Central in time for a shoot-out in front of the Legislative Council Building. Gulliver could have done it in Lilliput, crossing the harbour with a mere bound, but not normal-sized human beings, however fiendishly villainous. Nevertheless, we willingly suspend our disbelief because we recognise the conventions of the Jackie Chan yarn.

By contrast we can expect a more authentic depiction of Hong Kong (or indeed Macao) from Johnnie To. The question then must be, just how much more authentic is he? Why does a real sense of place matter in To's films? As Ackbar Abbas has pointed out, 'the new Hong Kong cinema deserves attention because it has finally found a worthy subject — it has found Hong Kong itself as a subject'.[1] To's major films of the last ten years succeed in framing the actions of groups and individuals within a clearly recognisable Hong Kong or Macao which is much more than a playground for enacting dramatic fantasy, and in many ways a secondary subject, as Abbas suggests. At the same time, how can such an elusive and disappearing subject (to refer to Abbas's proposition) be captured in fiction cinema in a way that relates to some sort of acknowledged reality without essentialising or trivialising it?

An equally pertinent question in the context of this chapter is this: why is it important to consider location and locale seriously, and is there anything to be gained by applying apparently spurious notions of authenticity in relation to location and locale? What is the difference between using location as playground, as discussed in the opening paragraph, and employing suggestive montage to create a bogus but aesthetically convincing sense of locale? After all, it could be argued that Hong Kong's art-house cinema (Wong Kar-wai's *Chungking Express*, for example) plays fast and loose with locale just as the Jackie Chan yarn does. Lawrence Pun's essay on Hong Kong location shooting in which he explores what he calls the 'emotional map of Hong Kong cinema' is very illuminating in this respect. He establishes a rationale for evaluating the emotional core of the film in the use of location, as 'the city in motion' is transformed into 'the stage of emotions'.[2] This stage of emotions is, as we shall see, intimately connected with the heart and soul of the film, in a similar way that stage space is integral to the stage play, where the stage is more than a place of action. Choices of location and locale are not as arbitrary as they sometimes appear in Hong

Kong cinema. However, this is not, as To has argued (see Appendix), a justification for pedantic objections on the basis of literal urban configurations and a director's refusal to adhere to them slavishly. For the non-local viewer, literal locale matters much less than an aesthetically consistent appearance of locale. In turn this has to do with directorial choices, which are aesthetically, even more than practically, motivated. Fundamentally what is important here is the artistic concept of *authenticating conventions* for a work of art, as in the theatre, and not factual authenticity.

This chapter will, therefore, contextualize the film *PTU* by discussing it in relation to its portrayal of Tsim Sha Tsui, the putative setting for the entire movie. Tsim Sha Tsui is in many ways a metonym for the wider Hong Kong community, but careful attention is given in the film to constructing a sense of locale, which feels like it has more in common with the concentration of a studio film set or theatrical stage set — the latter an analogy that To himself has acknowledged in interview. Talking of a division of the film into seven major scenes and the use of highly impressionistic stage-type lighting (see Appendix), he refers to the choice of quasi-theatrical perspectives in shot choice, which helped to create the distanced theatrical effect by contrast with the emotional closeness of the average movie. In view of its somewhat stage-like nature and its quality of heightened reality, the locus of the narrative events is more of a significant player than the specific locations used in most Hong Kong films.

As mentioned in the previous chapter, the film was difficult to complete, and this was for reasons not entirely unconnected with the setting and the location shooting. One considerable constraint on To's filming schedule was the necessity for night-time location shooting, which took place over a period of nearly two years, because it was felt that only Sunday nights between 2 a.m. and 6 a.m. would provide the right conditions, light quality and absence of people that To required in order to create the film's edgy and slightly eerie ambience at street level. Unsurprisingly, it was difficult to retain the sense of continuity for the project and in Hong Kong terms such seemingly inefficient shooting methods would normally be considered grotesquely self-indulgent and unreasonable. The whole point, according to the norms of the industry, is to shoot the film and wrap as quickly as possible, a pragmatic approach which rarely gives more than a vague impression of authentic location. Arguably, in most commercial films it does not matter too much. To chose not to conform to normal scheduling and as a result produced his most interesting depiction of milieu in any of his major films, a milieu in which time and space are compressed and flattened in typically cinematic and postmodern style. As we shall see in chapter 3, the consistency of the film's look and the visual continuity from one scene to the next are truly remarkable. Indeed, it is the consistency in direction and brilliance in the editing of the film that endow the film with this authenticity of setting, in spite of its poetic licence in terms of actual shooting location.

In order to appreciate the subject matter for To's filmic canvas, we should first take a closer look at the area of Kowloon that, narratively speaking, provides the setting for *PTU*. Tsim Sha Tsui — which literally means 'sharp sand-spit, a reference to its sandy promontory of earlier times' — is the main cultural and commercial district of Kowloon. Pun memorably describes it as 'the right ventricle' to Central's 'right atrium' at the city's very heart.[3] It is a bustling metropolitan district spread out over a radius of five square miles, part of the bigger Yau Tsim Mong (Tsim Sha Tsui–Yau Ma Tei–Mongkok) district with the busy Nathan Road, stretching from The Peninsula Hotel at one end to Prince Edward at the other, as its central axis. This 'golden mile' of Nathan Road is constantly busy, even in the small hours. It is a dazzling sequence of neon lights and bustling shop fronts and includes the famous Chungking Mansion (see Wong Kar-wai's filmic depiction of it in *Chungking Express*) among its many attractions. However, just off Nathan Road to the east, there is a network of streets — Cameron Road, Carnarvon Road, Granville Road, Kimberly Road, Mody Road, Hanoi Road and Minden Avenue — all humming with vitality most of the day and much of the night, but on account of the irregular, non-grid configuration of this area, arguably a little less salubrious than the Nathan Road thoroughfare. If one continues walking in an easterly direction one quickly arrives at Tsim Sha Tsui East, which is a palpably different, and more modern-looking district. The above-mentioned streets are the places one goes for a better bargain than one would find on Nathan Road generally speaking, and the area positively teems with factory outlet shops, which rub shoulders with cosmetics businesses and spatially compressed mobile-phone outlets. These streets also have their share of restaurants and other eateries, especially *tsa tsaan tengs* (literally 'tea-meal houses'). The area has moved inexorably up-market with yuppie developments like Knutsford Terrace and other trendy developments modelled on Central's SoHo stretch, but some of the intersecting streets in this area, for example Hanoi Road, have retained their rather dingy, down-at-heel ambience, especially late at night.

As the film opens the PTU team is set down at the start of their overnight shift close to the intersection of Carnarvon Road and Kimberly Road. The date is 14 September 2000 and the events of the film span the hours between the night of 14 September and the early hours of 15 September. In most cities it would be dark and quiet with only light from the street-lamps to illuminate the scene, but Hong Kong is not like most cities. The Yau Tsim Mong district remains animated and crowded until well after midnight. Attacks do occur in parts of Hong Kong, both in broad daylight and in the evening, but they are comparatively rare, usually confined to gang rivalries, and strikes are 'surgical', so to speak, and swift. Bystanders are very rarely embroiled in the violent settlement of gang turf disputes. By comparison with many world cities Hong Kong's streets are rather safe, although there was an upsurge in violent heists in the years preceding the 1997 handover, just as there was a marked increase in gangster gun battles surrounding territorial disputes on the streets of Macao in the twilight days of Portuguese rule. In general, however, people would normally not consider the streets of Hong Kong to be 'perilous' or indeed threatening, and there is much less danger of encountering desperate muggers or homicidal maniacs on the streets of Hong Kong than there is in the 'first world cities' of London, Paris or New York.

Still 7 Fanning out on the streets of Tsim Sha Tsui.

What is particularly interesting about To's film depiction of the vibrant Tsim Sha Tsui area is the depopulated look of the place. This can be contrasted sharply with other To films such as *Breaking News* or his recent 2007 film (wearing his producer's hat) *Eye in the Sky*, where the streets are positively teeming with people. The latter film is fundamentally about surveillance and the degree of anonymity that the crowd offers both police surveillance teams and miscreants. In these depictions crowded streets are therefore an integral part of the mise-en-scène. Not so, however, with *PTU* where all of the characters, major and minor, have their specific functions and roles to play, and there are relatively few extras, precisely because they are extraneous to dramatic requirements.

Interestingly his 2006 film *Exiled* depicts an even more depopulated Macao — one that looks like it has just experienced a *28 Days Later* type of scenario! Gang members await their target in a Macao street in which nobody, except their intended victim and a pusillanimously pragmatic off-duty cop, appears to come and go. In most of the subsequent scenes one would think that it is Day One of the Chinese New Year Holiday, a day when people stay home as a prelude to visits on succeeding days. Admittedly Macao has a smaller population than Hong Kong, but To appears to be recreating the ambience of a fly-blown, one-horse town as depicted in a Sergio Leone film, as opposed to a recognisable Macao side street. In the case of *PTU* there seems to be a more logical explanation, namely the cover of night. Since filming proceeded at slow pace over a two-year period exclusively in the pre-dawn hours of Sunday night to Monday morning — traditionally the quietest time of the week in these never-sleeping districts — it really was feasible to convey the impression of lonely locales. The SARS outbreak had nothing to do with such impressions of course, because by the time the short sharp shock of SARS descended upon Hong Kong, the film had already completed its post-production stage and was ready for general release in the territory.

In fact the earlier scenes of the film, despite connoting Tsim Sha Tsui locations, are spread more widely over Kowloon and indeed Hong Kong Island than even the long-term Hong Kong resident might suppose. Much of the footage of the Canton Road waterfront, for example, was actually shot at a quiet street intersection on the small island of Ap Lei Chau on Hong Kong side. In this connection To is a master of the cinematic illusion, or *trompe l'oeil* to borrow the theatrical term. The opening sequence, as we have seen, establishes the Tsim Sha Tsui location, despite the indeterminate departure point of the vehicle conveying the PTU unit to their place of duty. Having established this locus of the action, the director takes us to the Fong Wing Kee hot-pot restaurant in Kowloon City (supposedly within walking, or rather running distance of Tsim Sha Tsui). To's gastronomic interests as a filmmaker are legendary. More than most Hong Kong directors, he is concerned to represent one of the most culturally significant aspects of Chinese life, namely eating and drinking. There are few Chinese directors who can rival him in this aspect of cultural representation. Even in dramatic situations of great stress, for example in *Breaking News*, *Exiled* and *Election* there is at least one characteristic eating scene. In general one could describe the orality of eating and the tension it promotes while mental or social activity is subordinated to masticating and digesting, as more intrinsic to To's filmic world than the orality of talking. By the same token the oral satisfaction derived from eating and drinking is often portrayed positively as a panacea for stress and conflict. *PTU* is no exception to this tendency, although the technology of modern talking — especially that of the mobile phone — is also particularly foregrounded in the film. Not, incidentally, because To wishes to eulogise Hong Kong's all-pervasive and frequently fetishistic communication technology — with typical To irony he portrays the device from a far more ambivalent perspective than the average Hong Kong technophile would consider decent. The mobile phone, as we shall see in chapter 3, plays a significant if deceptive role in the film's plot. Eating, by contrast, is an essential and more straightforward activity, although even this is depicted in ambiguous terms, since both scenes of eating are disrupted, and the comfort and repose of a number of the 'happy eaters' profoundly disturbed.

As regards the Fong Wing Kee restaurant, it is used primarily because it is so nondescript and suggestive of a type. Such hot-pot restaurants — *for wor dim*, as they are called in Cantonese — are popular among Hong Kong locals and can easily be found in a busy commercial area, such as Tsim Sha Tsui. However, To's choice of the Fong Wing Kee may well have been related to reasons of convenience and suitability for filming. Whatever the reason, the restaurant's proximity to the Tsim Sha Tsui area is questionable for the purposes of any real-life spatial relations suggesting adjacency, as is the case with the film's patterns of signification. Put bluntly the travel time between Kowloon City and Tsim Sha Tsui is between fifteen and twenty minutes by taxi, private car or MTR. On foot, it would take at least an hour, possibly more. Not that real space and time matter too much in the representation of screen reality. However, it is clear from the film's signifying codes and conventions that the Fong Wing Kee is a short distance from the Tsim Sha Tsui alley where Sergeant Lo slips on his literal and metaphorical banana skin. This blurring of time and distance, which is a strong feature of the medium of cinema in general as well as of postmodernity as a contemporary condition, is, on the surface, unremarkable. One restaurant, it could be said, especially in Hong Kong, is pretty much like another restaurant.

Likewise the Chung Gwok Bing Sat in Mong Kok (close to Exit A of the MTR) is portrayed in the film as the place where the Police Tactical Unit enjoys a welcome food break during their dusk-to-dawn shift. The scene in this particular eatery is important since the place is used as a rendezvous point by the two sergeants (Lo and Ho) to discuss in as unobtrusive a manner as possible the next step to be taken. Their surreptitious *tête-à-tête* is rudely interrupted by Madam (Criminal Investigation Department [CID] Inspector Cheng, played by Ruby Wong) and her eager bloodhound-like 'boys', prompting Lo to make a surprisingly athletic dash for freedom, unhindered by Mike Ho's PTU colleagues. This 'Bing Sat' — literally, and formerly, iced drink shop, because such old restaurants originated in a more impoverished Hong Kong where owning a fridge was a luxury and if one wished to slake one's thirst the local 'Bing Sat' was the obvious place to repair to — is supposedly located in Tsim Sha Tsui, at least in our mental conceptualisation of the fictional space of the film. In fact there are still a number of such places in the Tsim Sha Tsui and Jordan area, so the film is not extending the bounds of credibility very far, except perhaps for those who recognise the specific locale where the scene is shot. For the requirements of the film scene, however, it was essential to shoot in a place that not only looked authentic (masquerading as an all-night restaurant) and basic in its décor, but crucially was on a split level with stairs and an appropriate exit for Lam Suet's dramatic flight from the implacable Ruby Wong.

Still 8 Two-shot in *bing sat/tsa tsaan teng*.

Postmodern conceptions of the modern city and modern life becoming overwhelmed by simulacra of formerly shared reality are very much evoked by To's pseudo-realistic settings and representations of Hong Kong space. This is a common feature of his film milieux, but with the possible exception of the Tsim Sha Tsui–set *Throw Down,* his evocation of setting is rarely so simultaneously 'real' and surreal, to the point where it becomes hyper-real. Teo has remarked on this aspect of *PTU* in his discussion of the look of the film:

> *PTU* thus takes place in a highly conceptual Kowloon where the distance from Kowloon City and Tsim Sha Tsui is a cinematic stone's throw. In this way, the film is a solid example of Kowloon Noir, a cine-geographic time frame that turns real locations and the action taking place within them into the subjective inner world

> of abstract action.... The 'real' in this instance is 'never more than a code of representation (of signification)', in Barthesian term ...[4]

The classic qualities of the film noir locale, as Teo points out, represent a fusion of the concrete and the abstract, the real and the mythic imaginary, working together to connote a dark image of the metropolis. In certain aspects, film noir can be said to have been influenced by the dark vision of expressionist cinema. Thus To's more noir films appear to aim for what one might call a visual poetry of street life in a highly imaginary personal space. It is of course precisely such a hyper-real, hyper-speed virtual reality that the youngsters in the memorable video games parlour scene inhabit. Thus, it is no coincidence that the PTU officers' enquiries about the whereabouts of the gangster Ponytail and by extension the location of Sergeant Lo's gun, which are mired in dramatically ironic misunderstanding, are frustrated by the sheer disconnectedness of the individuals and the bubbles of isolation in which they are immersed. This results in a farcical communications breakdown and, fortuitously, a surprise connection between Mike Ho and 'Fei Sa' via the unlikely medium of Ponytail's and his cousin's mobile phones.

For many people in Hong Kong, as in other big cities, the virtual spaces of the internet, of games fantasy worlds and of the mobile phone offer an alternative reality to the gritty, mundane working and living spaces inhabited by their parents' generation. Many of Hong Kong's shopping malls and public spaces are emblematic of that Deleuzean 'any-space-whatever' character of postmodern environments. The detached observer has the distinct impression of mental absence, of a dearth of meaningful social contact, connoting the sort of ungrounded feeling that Abbas has described in his study of Hong Kong's 'politics of disappearance', which deals at length with the cinematic representation of city space. Abbas makes a valid point about the relationship between disappearance and excessive visibility in his discussion of ways of seeing the city and its landmarks and architecture:

> Bilingual, neon-lit advertisement signs are not only almost everywhere; their often ingenious construction for maximum visibility deserves an architectural monograph in itself. The result of all this insistence is a turning off of the visual. As people in metropolitan centres tend to avoid eye contact with one another, so they now tend also to avoid eye contact with the city. When the visual becomes problematic because it is too complex, too conflicting, too unfamiliar, or too manipulative, then different ways of seeing the city — different scopic regimes — have to be brought into play.[5]

This problem in turn affects the representative scope of Hong Kong filmmakers whose subject, as Abbas observes, is Hong Kong itself, its institutions and its anxieties. How can such a complex and multi-layered vision — or mirage — be subtly and convincingly realised on screen without resorting to unsatisfying stereotypes and stock images?

Good examples of Abbas's notion of excessive visibility or not seeing what is in their field of vision (the Edgar Allan Poe idea in his story *The Purloined Letter*) abound in *PTU*. When Ponytail crashes the taxi he has attempted to drive to hospital in a vain attempt to save himself, his triad underlings run directly past him oblivious to everything but their desire to lead Lo on a wild goose chase. The crash, which would in normal circumstances elicit attention, seems to be none of their business, although ironically it is. Their lack of vision results in their being caged up and abused by Ponytail's father as punishment for their negligence. The lost gun itself would have been visible after the beating Lo received at the hands of Ponytail's gang, had the PTU patrol and the owner of the gun made even a perfunctory search for what was under their noses, instead of jumping to false conclusions. Of course it is the job of the police patrol to read the signs of the immediate environment in order to engage proactively, but the signs are often ambivalent and the significance of such signs can be confusing. Car alarms and broken car windows, a seemingly innocuous kid on a bicycle — these too are elements of the environment that may or may not be significant. But links between phenomena and events can often only be established with hindsight, and hindsight is of little use to the patrolling officers, who must concentrate their attention and vision on the here and now and on an accurate reading of the city's plethora of signs.

Still 9 Boy on bike.

To's representation of people's isolation is contrasted with the collective ethic of group dependency. Thus the two informers, who are beaten up by the CID men and the PTU officers respectively, are vulnerable in their individualism, as is Ponytail, who becomes an easy victim for the innocuous-looking, long-haired assassin in the hot-pot restaurant. Sergeant Lo is helpless as an individual in spite of his bullying bravado in the opening scenes. As he becomes aware of his own vulnerability and of the inexorability of events over which he appears to have little control, his sense of dependency on others including Mike Ho and Baldhead (Ponytail's vengeful father) increases dramatically. The depiction of Hong Kong, and

Tsim Sha Tsui in particular, as the sinister city of noir conventions and a place of isolation, as in Western noir films, is a little far-fetched as a creative conceit, and it is very much a reflection of To's consummate artistry as a director that we accept it and suspend our disbelief so completely. Not only is Hong Kong as an ethnically Chinese city culturally oriented towards the collective as opposed to the individualistic, the area between Tsim Sha Tsui and Mongkok is considered to be the most densely packed in the world. Apart from the obvious instances of solitary beggars and street sleepers in the city and other social outcasts, very few people appear to be cut off from the bustling communal heart of the city, and arguably even the apparently outcast seem more connected to the metropolitan centre than their Caucasian counterparts.

The opening sequence of the film, which presumably takes place from 8 p.m. onwards, given that the eight hours of action conclude at 4 a.m. in the Canton Road shoot-out, presents a slightly more social side of the city, but one which is not very authentic in its portrayal of Tsim Sha Tsui as we know it in actuality. Having said that, the film managed to achieve what was probably a felicitously accurate representation of most Hong Kong locales during the SARS period. Certainly, as the film progresses, the depiction of a communal sphere of activity fades away to be replaced by a much more stripped-down, depopulated and narrative-driven setting, akin perhaps to that of the typical modern stage play, in which only characters who have a clear dramatic function are present on stage. Such sparse, concentrated filmic visions of the city, are, as we have discussed above, integral to the aesthetic and the ambience of film noir, but film noir, unlike would-be realistic, drama-documentary-type creations, is more concerned with the city as emblem of an inner psyche, one that is affected by an often unspecified malaise. To's interest here, as with other of his films that analyse group instincts and individual motivation, is less focused on a totally authentic or realistic creation, but on one that, like film noir, has its own internal logic of space and cinematic composition. This is why any understanding or interpretation of the film, as we shall see in the final chapter, depends more on the internal, artistic logic and consistency of the film's theme and ideas than on an external, objective world beyond the cinematic frame.

To use the world of literature as an analogy, we must recognise that supposedly realistic depictions of specific and verifiably existing places, as in for example the novels of Balzac and Dickens, are only marginally more substantial in the reader's imagination than Jules Verne's mysterious islands, moonscapes and seascapes. Moreover, Verne's brief evocation of Hong Kong circa 1870 in *Around the World in Eighty Days*, as with the film depictions derived from the novel, is no more convincingly real than his extra-terrestrial descriptions. In other words, we are conscious of To's filmic evocation of the city as poetic crystallisation, as in the unreal, almost nightmarish Paris and London of Baudelaire's and Eliot's poetry. As with the creative visions of language poets who evoke cityscapes, more visually and conceptually sophisticated film directors like Johnnie To want to be creatively empowered to allude to what we know to be there without having their creativity restricted to a succession of literal photographic images. Our reading of the film's milieu must not therefore be based on a literal realism, in spite of the sometimes recognisable locations. If literal realism were important for To, one suspects he would make the street signs more distinct in the mise-en-scène of his films, instead of tending to shoot them obliquely, in such a way that we are unable to distinguish the street name with total certainty.

As Teo has observed, many To screenplays involve the use of rooftops, stairwells, lifts, dank passage-ways, escalators and other nondescript settings for the events depicted in his films.[6] Like Mak and Lau in *Infernal Affairs*, To loves to present the alienated, bird's eye view of the city or the distinctly blemished and non-photogenic side of its multi-faceted face. These approximate to the any-space-whatever that Deleuze has theorised so memorably in relation to cinematic evocation of postmodern space. However, there are relatively few interior scenes in *PTU* set in confined or claustrophobic spaces. The two major exceptions shock by their use of restricted or potentially dangerous space to convey both brutality and fear. Both scenes are positioned in the middle of the film. The first takes place in an ill-lit industrial building when the PTU officers are trying to locate Ponytail's gang and come across the girlfriends — possibly a euphemism for the street girls they pimp for — holed up in a cheerless temporary living quarter on one of the upper floors. The ascent of the stairs and shots of the stairwell are arguably redundant to the film's plot, at least from the perspective of what needs to be narrated. However it provides To with the opportunity to contrast the tight group ethos of the triad girlfriends and that of Mike Ho's subordinates, and at the same time provides a powerful image of the alienating, but very familiar, Hong Kong phenomenon whereby the unprepossessing industrial building is an intrinsic element in the city's psychic ambience.

Another industrial building is used by the gang led by Baldhead, and this one offers an even starker and more striking use of the open floor-space such buildings provide. Baldhead's own henchmen — much more ruthless, one realises, than Ponytail's gang of street punks — have incarcerated his son's inept acolytes, naked and shaven-headed in animal cages. The starkness of the setting and the raw, dehumanising savagery of Baldhead's violent blows on the bars of the cages make for a grim but unforgettable mise-en-scène, one that is skilfully created by the naturally oppressive ambience and depersonalised scale of the action set. Like any visually astute director, To captures the associations of the commonplace, soulless industrial building and imbues it with an intensified dramatic presence on screen. Watching his disturbing representation we are led to explore the darker recesses of our conscious and subconscious awareness of such places. Abbas has identified precisely such a

Freudian 'uncanny (*unheimlich*)' quality about places in Hong Kong: 'Changing cities produce many sights that are unfamiliar. But rapidly changing cities, cities without brakes like Hong Kong, produce something else as well: *the unfamiliar in the familiar* [his italics], that is the unfamiliar that is half seen, or seen subliminally behind the seen/scene of the familiar.'[7]

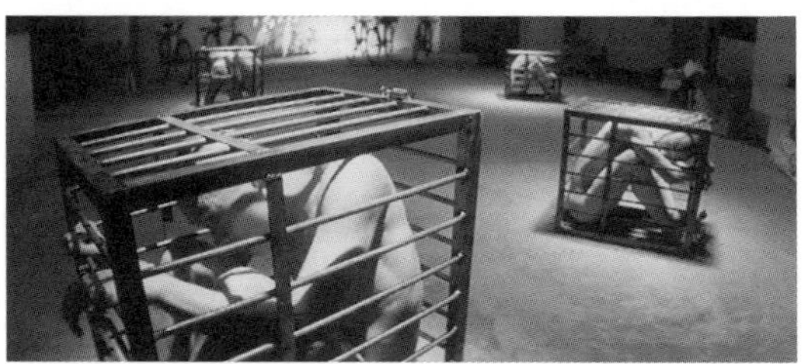

Still 10 Ponytail's boys in cages.

Of course we are familiar with the concept of 'the city as action set', whether in Hollywood movies or Hong Kong 'heroic bloodshed' films. In such frequently superficial evocations of milieu, everything else, including character development, artistic verisimilitude, narrative and spatial logic, the sense of environment and community, is entirely subordinated to the idea of city places as functional backdrops for one hectic action scene after another. In the typical commercial vehicle, such as Jackie Chan's *Rush Hour* series or the *Die Hard* franchise, the film action moves in predatory fashion through the city appropriating its milieu purely for the purposes of the visceral, unearned screen thrill. By sharp contrast, a carefully researched and intelligently wrought police thriller, such as Peter Weir's 1986 film *Witness*, relies considerably on its creation of ambience and environment to generate and authenticate the film's unfolding action. Likewise,

Roman Polanski's 1990 thriller *Frantic* succeeds in conveying a sense of an utterly hostile and defamiliarised Paris in which an increasingly desperate Harrison Ford roams the streets and the banks of the Seine hoping to discover some sign of the whereabouts of his abducted wife. The filmmaking process transforms a habitual environment, synonymous with tourist spectacle and romance, into a baleful and ultimately frustrating milieu, a million miles from the vast majority of Parisian representations. Thus, casting the city or rural location as action set does not preclude it from playing an intrinsic role, as opposed to an utterly irrelevant one, in the construction of the movie's referential world. Too many Hong Kong films play fast and loose with Hong Kong's own identity, not because they take poetic licence in their geographical conceptualisation of place, which is, as we have seen, inherent in any poetics of cinema, but because they treat the city so casually, almost as a super-real but strangely cardboard studio set. Such films deny the possibility that Hong Kong itself can be construed as an element worthy of filmic depiction. To tends to be offhand about the significance of place in his films, stressing the logistics and pragmatics involved in the difficult business of location shooting. Notwithstanding his protestations about the necessity for a strictly utilitarian approach to such things (see Appendix), I believe *PTU* represents, among other things, a homage to the social and historical significance of locale in the appreciation of film. In that sense local films such as *PTU* (one could also cite Stanley Kwan's *Rouge* and *Island Tales*, Mabel Cheung and Alex Law's *City of Glass*, and Wong Kar-wai's *Chungking Express* and *In the Mood for Love*) run counter to the trend of much current commercial cinema.

Police, guns and triads

In addition to being something of a homage to the Hong Kong locale, the film offers a well-researched and thus realistic depiction of aspects of the Hong Kong police, including their use of weapons. Unlike some police forces, and it would be invidious to give current examples, the Hong Kong police force does not, fortunately, have the reputation of being trigger-happy, or of shooting first and asking questions afterwards. As a developed modern city in which the rule of law prevails, the idea of the Hong Kong police shooting down innocent bystanders or attacking political protestors, a common phenomenon in a depressingly large number of other societies, is inconceivable. To's interest in making a film about the PTU, according to comments made in interview, goes back at least ten years prior to the film's release in 2003, and it is clear from the result that he did his research conscientiously and with passion for the subject. Whilst one does not wish to paint too rosy a picture, To's films generally depict the police as doing a professional job in sometimes difficult circumstances. In many of his films, for example *The Longest Nite* and *Running Out of Time*, a dichotomous image is conveyed, whereby the police and criminals are portrayed as fundamentally dependent on and complementary to each other, much as in Melville's crime dramas. To has commented in interview (DVD Cantonese language interview) that cops and robbers are mirror images of each other, and in *The Longest Nite* in particular he conveys this metaphor quite literally in one of the closing scenes. In *PTU* the relationship is explored with greater subtlety, and the default position is that the police are the good guys, since the point of view adopted in the film's narrative is primarily theirs. As we shall see in chapter 4, To pushes this idea to the limit, and asks questions of the viewer in his representation of the police and their methods. Although many Hong Kong films in the period subsequent to the 1997 handover have explored this dichotomous relationship

— most famously *Infernal Affairs* — it is true to say that none have approached the subject in as much depth and with as much ironic perspicacity as To.

Of course, like many other police forces, the Hong Kong Police — formerly the Royal Hong Kong Police — is not without its skeletons in the closet. The British Police Force, on which it was to a considerable extent modelled, endured some worrying scandals in recent memory. Not least of these were the murky 'Stalker affair' of the 1970s and the British Police and Army links to the Royal Ulster Constabulary's unacknowledged 'shoot-to-kill' policy in Northern Ireland. For the Hong Kong Police force its darkest hour was probably in the corruption-ridden years of the 1950s and 60s, when bribes, backhanders and protection money (so-called tea money) were a routine part of the job. This corruption permeated through every level of the force from the top down and a number of high-ranking officers, notably the cynical British Superintendent Peter Godber, were eventually caught and punished, after vast unexplained sums were discovered in their bank accounts. The formation of the Independent Commission Against Corruption in 1974 was a major step in counteracting such endemic corruption in the Territory's police, and since the nadir of the 1960s, the reputation of the Hong Kong Police has slowly and steadily risen. Whether or not they justify the reputation of the nickname bestowed upon them by one influential journalist, 'Asia's Finest', and whether this is mere hyperbole, are open to debate. However what is indisputable is that the police force of today is generally held in better esteem by the population of Hong Kong than it was previously. Cases of alleged police torture of suspects have been documented, in some cases leading to disciplinary action of officers found guilty of an excess of zeal, to put it euphemistically, but these are comparatively rare.

Many Hong Kong filmmakers have charted the vicissitudes of earlier decades, however, including veteran martial arts director Ng Ma, whose 1988 film *The Story of Kennedy Town* foregrounded the whole issue of corruption and duplicity by police officers in Hong Kong. More recent police dramas, especially those involving Jackie Chan's participation, have tended to present more positive depictions, often depending on whether or not the police officers roles are conceived as star vehicles. To's films up to *PTU*, with the exception of *Expect the Unexpected*, had not offered the kind of group character study of a public body that was attempted in, for example, *Lifeline*. Unlike *Lifeline*, in which all — even the protocol-driven senior management — are portrayed through a sympathetic lens, Hong Kong people's residual ambivalence about their police force, or at least the force's past misdemeanours, is skilfully conveyed in *PTU*. As we shall see in the final chapter, To is more preoccupied with contemporary issues in his nuanced representation.

The titular Police Tactical Unit appears to consist of normal police officers in every particular, except for their distinctive blue berets. In other respects they resemble the green- (summer) or blue- (winter) uniformed police officers on duty throughout the city. Formed as far back as 1956 after an emergency connected with the Double 10th riots — the 10 October celebration of the founding of the Kuomintang Republic (not of the People's Republic, which is 1 October) when Hong Kong–based factions supporting Taiwan and the Republic of China respectively frequently clashed over such public shows of allegiance before the 1990s — the Police Tactical Unit was founded to operate in situations requiring crowd management and control, anti-crime operations, threats to internal security and also in the event of natural disasters. Originally housed in temporary Nissan shelters in Fanling in the New Territories — many of which were a lot less temporary than intended — the PTU now have their own headquarters, where recruits are put through a programme of exacting professional training. Although Fanling is still their base, PTU officers are deployed to patrol different parts of the city, especially when unusual events call for their specialist intervention. During the December 2006 World Trade Organization (WTO) meeting in Hong Kong, for example, the PTU would certainly have been used to prevent activists gaining access to the Hong Kong Convention and Exhibition Centre where the spectacularly expensive and unsuccessful world trade negotiations were being conducted, in view of their expertise in the area of security. This expertise and readiness for active duty and potentially dangerous situations is predicated on rigorous levels of training and meticulous attention to detail.

When normal conditions prevail on the streets of Hong Kong, Police Tactical Unit patrols are deployed on street patrol, but they are also frequently used to back up ordinary police officers in emergency situations, such as that recounted in *PTU*, in which a mainland gang is on the loose after a bloody heist. Each of the six PTU companies comprises 1,020 officers. The companies are subdivided into platoons, each platoon comprising 32 officers (male and female) with eight sergeants, reporting to a senior station sergeant. Also attached to the PTU is the Special Duties Unit (or SDU), founded in 1974 and modelled very closely on the British Special Forces, which offers specialist support including sniper operations. The PTU patrol depicted in the film is presumably part of a mainstream PTU company, and not affiliated to the SDU, although the officers' sharp-shooting skills, as portrayed in the film's climactic sequence, are reasonably authentic, given the PTU's and SDU's emphasis on the highest levels of relevant professional training and the strictest discipline. In addition to their utterly distinctive blue berets, which are worn with pride, PTU policemen wear heavy-duty boots as opposed to the flat shoes of the regular force, making them look something of a hybrid — both policeman and commando.

Still 11 PTU officers.

The Organised Crime and Triad Bureau (the OCTB), which also features prominently in To's and other directors' films, is responsible, as the name implies, for monitoring triad-related crime in the HKSAR. Included in its remit is the control and prevention of smuggling, of vice rings and of syndicated, unlicenced gambling in Hong Kong. Its activity is focused particularly on the movements of triad societies and their close connections with organised crime. The bureau is supported by the work of the Criminal Intelligence Bureau (CIB), which gathers intelligence about such criminal groups. This latter bureau has developed links with mainland anti-crime forces and the increased incidence of shared intelligence of more recent years has borne fruit in terms of the sharp reduction in the type of violent robberies and territorial in-fighting, which terrorised the Hong Kong and Macao populations in the 1990s. By contrast the Criminal Investigation Department (CID) has its roots in the British police system. Its work is obviously related to that of the OCTB and CIB, and the kind of inter-unit rivalry, suggested by To's portrayal of the nature of the working relationship across the various groups, is by no means pure fiction. As the film shows, however, the default position may be competitive and mistrustful, but when external threats manifest themselves in the shape of well-armed criminals, a spirit of co-operation and mutual respect emerges. An important maxim that the events of the film foreground is that 'all those who wear the same uniform are part of the family', which inevitably invites comparisons with the notions of 'family' that are inherent in the triad tradition. Fascinatingly, the Chinese god Kwan Yu who symbolises the quality of *yee hei* (brotherhood/loyalty) is the patron god of both police and triads.

Naturally, another way of looking at it is that the police tend to close ranks in the face of any outside threat, whether an armed criminal challenge or a legitimate civil enquiry into their conduct. Investigators into the racist attitudes deep-rooted in the British Metropolitan Police force, in the wake of the infamous Stephen Lawrence murder cover-up, encountered stubborn resistance to widespread suggestions of the need for transparency and change. By comparison, the Hong Kong Police force has not been affected by such high-level public scandal since the early 1970s and the corruption business, at least not until the Tsim Sha Tsui underground shoot-out between three police officers in March 2006. The police enquiry into the incident was quick to exonerate two of the officers involved, one of whom, Wilson Sin Ka-keung, survived his wounds. Two of the officers were subsequently awarded a police medal for bravery in attempting to apprehend the third. There was a certain amount of scepticism in the media about the speed with which the police internal investigation concluded that dead cop Tsui Po-ko, aged thirty-five, was a single rotten apple, and some commentators suggested that there was a clear need to extend the scope of enquiries into gambling debt and other problems among junior policemen. Furthermore the view was expressed that the gallantry awards might have been better delayed until after the deliberations of the public inquest, scheduled for a later date, since they might be seen as prejudicial to the outcome. The 2001 murder of fellow policeman Leung Shin-yan was also attributed to Tsui. It was seen as a premeditated act designed to procure the latter's gun for use in a bank robbery, in which he later shot dead security guard Zafar Iqbal Khan. The public inquest into these events, which took place in early 2007, predictably absolved the police force from blame and identified Tsui Po-ko as the sole miscreant in the affair.

The gun that Tsui had appropriated for his misdeeds was the standard police issue Smith and Wesson Colt Detective Special, calibre .38. This gun has a long history of production going back to 1927, but since 1986 the semi-automatic weapon has been unavailable, as production was discontinued after that year. As a 2006 report in the *South China Morning Post* indicated, the decision to update the standard Hong Kong police weapon and tender for a new model encountered an obstacle, in that the requested specifications provided by various police bodies proved unrealistic and impractical.[8] In the film *PTU*, the now obsolete Smith and Wesson Colt is the gun that causes such consternation to its owner by disappearing temporarily. For a police officer to lose his gun is a serious disciplinary offence, and the natural instinct for an officer, such as the murdered Leung Shin-yan, would be to grapple with any assailant who attempted to take it from him. When 'Fei Sa' Lo realises that his is missing his first instinct is to instigate a covert search and prevent report of its loss by prevailing on his PTU buddy, Mike Ho. Subsequently he visits a toy replica store (awaking its ruffled but uncomplaining owner in the middle of the night) and, after sawing off the barrel of the purchased replica to fit the 51 mm specified length and spraying it regulation black, sticks it in his gun holster. When the shooting starts he instinctively goes for his Smith and Wesson until comically the realisation dawns on him that it is unlikely to be of much use in a real fire-fight. In the same fire-fight the PTU patrol all use a different weapon from Sergeant Lo. Their handguns differ not only in possessing real fire-power, but also in respect of the model, which is more refined with greater capability. Also made by Smith and Wesson, the .40 calibre military police pistol has fifteen bullets to the Colt's mere six, and is double the latter gun's barrel length. The distance between the PTU patrol and their criminal targets is considerable, and the latter are clearly armed with much heavier weaponry. However the PTU's lighter but accurate handguns, in combination with their iron discipline and faster reactions, help them to prevail in the exchange of fire. By contrast the gunplay of the rival local triad bosses Baldhead and Eyeball is less authentic, and more like a parody of the shoot-out scene in an old Hollywood western. Teo points out the intertextual associations of To's gunplay action films to the romantic-chivalric *wuxia* and the '"urban Western", which is a form conducive to gender-specificity and to guns and violence', but maintains that 'To's action films are implicitly different from the Western in both a cultural and generic sense'.[9]

The Hong Kong triads are depicted in less farcical and more sinister hues in To's next movie *Election*, a representation more in keeping with the image of an international or regional criminal network, similar to that evoked by films such as the *Infernal Affairs* trilogy and Derek Yee's 2006 film *The Protégé*. The comparison and contrast effects that To wished to create in *PTU* between the local triads, the mainland gang and the various police units perhaps resulted in the downplaying of the rival triads' significance, particularly in the shoot-out where their bitter struggle and mutual elimination of the two senior figures is ironically reduced to a ridiculous side-show. As many other films, not least Johnnie To works, have demonstrated, established Hong Kong triad groups such as the Sun Yee On and the 14K (which I naively mistook for the number of a bus in my early years in Hong Kong — I waited for it, but fortunately for me it never arrived) have often acted with ruthless disregard for public safety and with a kind of obsessive tit-for-tat motivation that can threaten the stability and reputation of the city. However, it is also true to say that a certain stasis exists in Hong Kong, a tacit agreement whereby triad 'business activities' are contained within normative parameters, and whilst there is ongoing surveillance of their activities, a certain level of pragmatic co-existence, often based on macho posturing, has been achieved, as the wily Lo's antics in the first part of the film show. Certainly at the higher levels of the police force the desire to crack down on and ultimately eradicate illegal triad operations, such as drug smuggling, loan sharking, 'protection' racketeering, illicit gambling and prostitution, is genuine. At the same time there is a realistic recognition within the police force as a whole of the sheer scale of the problem. The police have been arguing for increased powers to combat organised crime, and especially for stronger laws including an Organised and Serious Crimes Bill to be passed by the SAR's legislative body.[10]

The triads started out in the eighteenth century as patriotic political societies dedicated to the overthrow of the Manchu Qing Dynasty in China, hence the strong traditions of brotherhood and honour in these organisations. It is estimated by the Police (website) that approximately fifty different groups of triads, of greater and lesser importance, are currently active in Hong Kong. The conceit that all triads are mystically linked and unified in one invincible super-organisation is a myth that helps to consolidate their power bases and frighten law-abiding members of the community into ignoring the social blight brought about by organised crime. Despite attempts to infiltrate and close down triad organisations, their long-held codes of secrecy and silence have proved difficult to break down. Unlike the gangs of desperadoes who arrive with lightning speed from the mainland and strike with deadly efficiency and callous disregard for human life, the triads tend to be more cautious about disrupting social order, partly because it is commonly regarded as being bad for business. In *PTU* To is interested in the relationship between police and triads at a time of crisis for both parties, when the advent of a third element — the mainland raiders — upsets the equilibrium of the equation. His exploration of professionalism and group ethos is central to the realistic issues and themes that the film presents, but so too is his implicit critique of myth and propaganda associated with the rhetoric and self-image of both organisations. The mainland gang, as the film depicts both symbolically and graphically, impinges on Hong Kong's consciousness and challenges its sense of security and its status quo. It has little interest in the codes of behaviour, customs and territorial pacts of Hong Kong–based 'black-hand' organisations. Thus the dualism of police and triads is radically altered. The survival instinct of both groups would normally prompt them to do business — at least temporarily — with mainland counterparts, as films like *Election* and *Infernal Affairs* depict, but in *PTU* and *Breaking News* there is little or no room for negotiation, and only violence can resolve the impasse.

3

'Expect the Unexpected' – *PTU*'s Narrative and Aesthetics

'From the 1970s to the 1990s, as Hollywood was establishing intensified continuity as its major stylistic norm, Hong Kong directors picked up on it and revised it in key ways ... Such sequences have counterparts in the work of Tsui Hark, Corey Yuen, Sammo Hung, Johnnie To and many others, and they show that filmmakers steeped in a tradition of expressive movement could adapt changing international norms to their own purposes.'

— David Bordwell, *Transcultural spaces: Towards a Poetics of Chinese Film*

'A history of forms will always be an experimental history, not an empirical one, because it is aiming at something that animates (often in a subterranean way) the work of filmmakers – some impulse that is going to emerge and develop unevenly, surprisingly, in particular movies or "runs" of movies. So, the impulse towards a certain kind of action-painting in cinema – not driven primarily by literary constructs of character or theme, or ideological processes, but a more abstracted form of action as

> screen sensation — is what I am calling a Hong Kong style. In Hong Kong cinema itself it runs roughly from King Hu to Johnnie To, and has, despite the gloomy prognoses of naysayers, not yet finished evolving.'
>
> — Adrian Martin, 'At the Edge of the Cut' in *Hong Kong Connections*

Preamble: To's aesthetics in *PTU*

In this chapter we will explore the film's plot and story as well as its mise-en-scène and the aesthetic principles underlying its composition. As one internet evaluation put it rather whimsically, *PTU* must be 'the best film there is about a bunch of men walking in the street' (http://www.naturalbornviewers.com/archive/p/ptu/review.htm). This is not purely a tongue-in-cheek comment, since the film's edgy narrative and forward propulsion rely on the simple device of following the police patrol on the beat, which has its own kinetic logic. As To has indicated in interview (see Appendix) the relationship between stasis and movement in film is for him an ideal property of his chosen field of creative work. In the case of *PTU* this crucial balance between the two is achieved with great flair. To a considerable extent, of course, it is greatly facilitated by the natural rhythm of the subject matter. In other words, the film's narrative and aesthetic concept, its movement-images and action-images, to refer to Deleuzean film theory, are predicated on the tempo of the police street patrol's progress through the 'perilous night' of Tsim Sha Tsui. Movement is arrested at significant moments, and at two appropriate points of the narrative slow motion is intelligently and subtly deployed to achieve precisely that stillness within motion that To aspires to capture in his cinematic aesthetic.

David Bordwell's analysis of the poetics of Hong Kong cinema is helpful. He makes many illuminating points about Hong Kong's cinematic style and refers specifically to Johnnie To among others in his exegesis. Much of what he says about rhythm and expressive movement applies to To's aesthetics:

> For one thing Hong Kong filmmakers, probably drawing from indigenous Chinese traditions of theatre and martial arts, have developed a rhythmic conception of expressive movement that builds on the sheerly visceral aspect of cinema's appeal. By presenting a cleanly delineated piece of action, framed at the beginning and end by a slight pause, Hong Kong filmmakers have created a distinctive staccato rhythm. This is, in turn, amplified by colour, music, editing, framing and other film techniques.[1]

However, Bordwell goes on to discuss the ratio of tight close-ups and medium close-ups as well as accelerated cutting rates and faster shot speed in relation to his application of the concept of 'intensified continuity' to Hong Kong films and thence to global action cinema. Interestingly *PTU* goes against the grain by decelerating the average shot speed considerably, extending the length of scenes way beyond the norm for so-called action cinema and utilising relatively few close-ups. This is done for narrative, aesthetic and ideological reasons that will be more fully expounded in the present chapter and in chapter 4. As Bordwell aptly observes, directors like To adapt stylistic devices like intensified continuity idiosyncratically according to their own requirements. This is especially evident in his use of 'the prowling camera', which is intrinsic to the composition and narrative technique of *PTU*.

Still 12 Wide shot of crashed car on street corner and police investigating Ponytail's corpse.

With further reference to the film's visual style, I would like to pick up on Adrian Martin's perceptive allusion to what he calls 'action-painting' in the quotation at the opening of this chapter. Like To's follow-up film *Throw Down*, *PTU* has a strongly pictorial quality, which reveals the director's acute sense of visual aesthetics. In interview To discussed the affinity of his filmic composition in the two films to the aesthetics of traditional Chinese painting, emphasising elements such as mist and rain and creating a feeling that is also captured in some old films. Indeed, it is quite remarkable that at whatever point one pauses the DVD version of the film one is struck by the compositional skill and painting-like richness in detail of the image and the sheer beauty of To's mise-en-scène. As with *Throw Down*, the colour schemes and brilliant chiaroscuro effects seem to emanate from a painter's palette as much as from a filmmaker's eye for composition. Both films on the large screen were coincidentally beautiful to look at, but of course one's expectations of a Hong Kong film lead one to concentrate on 'action' and 'what happens next' more than look, so it is not until the DVD pause button is pressed that the virtuosic use of colour — steely blue and iridescent green in particular — and of varied and symbolically suggestive perspective, framing and subject distribution can be fully appreciated by the viewer. Add to these effects a highly effective use of wide-angle shots to include street detail and a lighting scheme that varies from garishly neon-lit to extremely noir at appropriate points with dark spaces at the edge of the frame and spotlights on pockets of visual interest in the centre of the frame, and you begin to see why To is such a master of cinema. Equally one must give enormous credit to the luminous cinematography of Cheng Siu-keung. The latter realizes To's directorial vision and artistic taste with a matching skill and subtlety that suggests considerable collaborative empathy between the two. Yet another striking aspect of the cinematography is of course the relatively low proportion of close-up shots in *PTU*, which has the effect of distancing the viewer emotionally. Thus, unlike more melodramatic and sentimental filmic devices which encourage the viewer to engage and empathise with the protagonists' point of view, desires and emotional responses, To's and Cheng's approach to the camera is to allow it to operate in a voyeuristic but estranged way, with comparatively few point-of-view close-ups. This approach discourages the viewer from engaging too closely on an emotional level with any of the characters.

The film's aesthetics are coloured by its chiaroscuro lighting effects and intensified colour schemes, which bathe the Tsim Sha Tsui locations in eerie yellowish-greenish hues with visual ingenuity and a distinct sense of hyper-reality. The visual stimuli of the film's cinematography evoking grungy, deserted streets and of the thoughtfully symmetrical elements in the mise-en-scène engage the viewer totally in a visually suggestive spectacle. The viewer constantly needs to respond constructively to the visual elements of the film, as opposed to simply working out where the narrative is going. Thus he or she is put in the shoes of the PTU officers as they try to comprehend the scene and anticipate possible attacks or danger that they may be about to walk right into. Moreover, the field of vision at night, as we know, is different from that of day, and the cat-like alertness exhibited by the officers (Sergeant Kat — appropriately enough — in particular) enhances tension, as we see the threats posed by the shadowy street environment to some extent through the PTU officers' eyes. Indeed, the palpable sense of night that the film's cinematography conveys to the viewer contributes a phenomenologically authentic feel to each scene. In so doing it attenuates the tentative and unpredictable narrative development, which is intended to emphasise the uncertainties that are a policeman's 'unhappy lot' (to paraphrase W. S. Gilbert's libretto for *The Pirates of Penzance*) between the hours of dusk and dawn. Finally, the diegetic street sound in the film is crucial to the creation of an attenuated sensibility. It functions as both a narrative and an aesthetic component, drawing the viewer in more closely as a listener. The PTU officers rely as much on their ears as on their eyes for information. Any sound could be potentially significant. Thus the prevailing mood of nocturnal vigilance is strongly enhanced by the film's combination of diegetic street-sound and non-diegetic ambient music, both skilfully employed to complement the visual aesthetics of the film.

The film: Frame by frame

PTU's plot strands and subjects may be summarised as follows and we will explore the way they are interwoven in the frame-by-frame analysis of the film that this section presents:

1. The mainland robbers
2. Ponytail and his gang
3. The PTU unit
4. Sergeant Lo and the missing gun
5. CID Inspector Cheng and the triad murder mystery
6. Triad gang rivalry of Baldhead and Eyeball
7. Mysterious kid on a bicycle

The exposition: Life's banana-skins

As the film opens we hear the diegetic soundtrack of street noises, car engines and beeping horns, etc. Then in combination with the opening image of a neon-lit street scene framed through the grille at the rear of a police truck, we hear a news report on the radio about a bank heist in North Point on Hong Kong Island. According to the news item HK$18 million was stolen and the lone police officer who attempted to intervene was shot through the head and was subsequently pronounced dead. The officers sitting on either side of the police van, whose faces are coming more clearly into focus, become quite animated in discussing the event, with one asserting that he knew the dead officer. As the lame sexual jokes about the officer's widow begin to exceed the bounds of decency, the quietly commanding presence of Sergeant Mike Ho (Ho Man Tsin) is felt in the first medium close-up on him, as he sits slightly apart from the others sunk in private thoughts. Pricking up his ears at this talk, Ho reprimands the group for their ill-timed levity by pointing out with firmness and dignity that 'anyone who wears the uniform is one of our own'. This motif is taken up later in the film. A second voice, that of a woman — Sergeant Kat, as we soon discover — reduces the potential for tension with the mediating remark that 'whatever happens, nothing beats returning home safely'. This is the second motif which underpins the film's narrative idea, and it is significant that it should be Kat who expresses such a non-heroic but pragmatic sentiment. Thus in this economical opening sequence we are introduced to not only characters and essential back-story, but also to slightly conflicting values and attitudes between the more experienced sergeants and the more 'gung-ho' young subordinates. The officers' blue berets, which betoken the PTU as opposed to the regular police, constitute not only a recurring emblem of group identity but also a strangely tactile feature for the camera to pick up on and highlight. With their metallic blue sheen and dimpled texture the berets somehow impinge constantly on our consciousness in virtually every scene in which the PTU officers appear.

Still 13 Simon Yam in truck — opening frame.

This masterly exposition establishes what we need to know extremely economically, but of course as viewers we are still attuning ourselves to the ambience of the film, and at this stage we do not know exactly what we need to know. It is easy to miss the vital detail of the bank robbery, which means of course that in the final sequence of the film one is taken as much by surprise by the appearance of the gang of desperadoes as the PTU officers are. By emphasising the information about the murdered police officer in the ensuing banter among the young officers and lecture from Mike, the screenplay skilfully distracts us from focusing on the heist. This means that the mainland gang functions both as a tight plot component with a logically motivated role and also as a surprise element in the film's carefully controlled, but seemingly arbitrary dénouement. As the truck arrives at its destination and drop-off point in the Kimberly Road area, close to Carnarvon Road — the network of streets connecting the two main thoroughfares of Nathan Road and Chatham Road — the film's hauntingly effective soundtrack music chimes in, consisting principally of guitar (with lots of echoing 'reverb') and bass. The feel of the music is restrained but simultaneously tense and spare. Its non-diegetic quality blends perfectly with the diegetic soundtrack elements, composed of authentic ambient street sounds. At this point the film's title appears in metallic blue against a black background with each of the three letters spot-lit in turn, connoting the act of torch-assisted surveillance, which indeed anticipates the scene in the stairwell of an industrial building approximately half-way through the film.

Following the film's title and opening credits, we are introduced to the other principal participants in the night's events arriving at a hot-pot restaurant supposedly in Tsim Sha Tsui, but actually located in Kowloon City to the north-east. We see Ponytail (a fashion item for men in Hong Kong that was popularised here by the ponytail sported by classy Italian footballer Roberto Baggio) and his triad 'street-punk' boys sauntering across the street, oblivious to passing taxis, which is a wonderfully ironic touch in view of his desperate need for one very shortly afterwards, and entering the restaurant in a swaggeringly proprietorial manner. The camerawork is already detached and observational — ironically so — rather than emotionally engaging, and this strategy is maintained more or less throughout the film, although there are a number of brief emotional reaction shots to events. Tight close-ups, which are intended to enhance the spectator's engagement with characters, are largely avoided, however. The triad's arrogant, intimidatory behaviour causes both manager and customers to treat them circumspectly. A farcical game of musical chairs and tables ensues when it transpires that the only table available is placed underneath a dripping air-conditioner. The apologetic manager moves a nerdy-looking and innocuous, long-haired customer in a Hawaiian shirt to another table in order to accommodate the wrathful Ponytail, on whom the offending air-conditioner has dripped copiously. The disgruntled Ponytail and his cronies are moved to the bigger table and the weedy young man, carrying his shopping bag in the manner of a housewife in a wet market, is moved to smaller one.

Still 14 Depth shot of separate tables — Ponytail, Lo etc.

The film then cuts to the exterior of the hot-pot restaurant, as we see anti-triad police officer Sergeant Lo Sa — Fei Sa to his friends and colleagues (the good-humoured Lam Suet, who in my view is chubby rather than fat, is always typecast as 'fatty' in To's films, but does not seem to mind!) — arrive in his car and park outside. After a brief altercation with another street punk offering 'parking service', after which Lo is described as 'an arrogant bastard', he in turn saunters into the restaurant and a territorial power contest takes place. The medium close-ups on Lo and Ponytail express this grudging sense of tacit agreement for a kind of 'cold-war' balance of power. The concept of balance that the restaurant scene cleverly evokes is of crucial importance for the later events of the night that so spectacularly upset this relatively stable co-existence of group interests in the Hong Kong context. That the macho posturing and subsequent accommodation are viewed through a farcical-ironic lens is typical of To's directorial perspective. Lo's aggressively confrontational act of plonking himself down at Ponytail's newly acquired big table and 'psyching out' his angry subordinates makes a clear statement about his dominion, one that Ponytail has too much 'savvy' to challenge in public despite the superiority in numbers on his side. After an exchange of cigarette smoke and mean looks all round, Ponytail orders his gang to move to 'Hawaiian shirt's' table and the harassed manager, apologising profusely for the dripping air-conditioner, reseats the solitary young man. In all, the farce of 'musical chairs and tables' occurs three times, which is exactly the same number of times as the confusing farce of mobile phones that follows, as well as being the number of coincidences in general that occur in the opening sequences of the film. In comedy, as in many other cultural contexts, repetition and the numerology of three are both conventional devices and To employs them here naturalistically and skilfully, but also with devastatingly understated whimsical humour. This humour is achieved visually and aurally (through diegetic sound) rather than by means of dialogue. The three tables are shot with a strong sense of depth and spatial framing, making it clear to the viewer that they are the primary foreground subjects and the customers on other tables merely background. Each of the mobile phones, Motorola models with identical ring-tones, rings in fairly close succession, thereby causing all three of the parties to take out their phones three times. The coincidence of the three phones ringing one after the other, each time for a different call recipient, is the first coincidence, but one that does not stretch the bounds of credibility too far. Sitting at adjacent tables in a restaurant normatively imposes a sense of social decorum and a minimum standard of social convention, and the humour derives from our implicit knowledge of the situation, as well as the faint air of absurdity that To's visual humour lends it. At the same time the situation is entirely credible and presented as such, since the film's treatment of this and other humorous moments studiously avoids the over-the-top, contrived effects common to the established local genres of comedy. In that sense To's darkly distanced humour is very un–Hong Kong, in that it seeks a grim humour in actuality, a humour born of social, political and even philosophical scepticism, I would argue.

First Ponytail's phone call informs him that his boys should check on 'Star River' — we are never informed whether this refers to a real place or a race-horse, or something less legitimate — which conveniently removes Ponytail's four punk bodyguards. The second call, which has Ponytail and the furtive-looking 'Hawaiian shirt' both scrambling for the mobiles once more, is for Lo, who leaves his food half-finished and exits the restaurant. The third is for 'Hawaiian shirt' and is his signal to assassinate Ponytail, which he does with startlingly unceremonious dispatch, taking out a big restaurant kitchen knife from his shopping bag and planting it with surprising force in the unsuspecting Ponytail's back. Ironically, in order to get away from the dripping air conditioner, Ponytail had re-seated himself conveniently close to the assassin facing away from him, in other words making himself a sitting target. This act, incidentally, constitutes coincidence number two. Ponytail's face as he realised he is seriously wounded is a comic picture. As the long-haired killer flees through the kitchen, Ponytail staggers out of the front door with the knife still sticking out of his back. Unable to hail a taxi at first, he eventually gets into the back seat of one, as the previous occupant alights. When the horrified taxi driver becomes aware of the nature of his new 'fare', he abandons his taxi with alacrity and flees from the scene. Ponytail has no option but to attempt to drive it himself to the nearest hospital, and clambers painfully into the driver's seat. As regards the cinematography at this point, the chiaroscuro effects of lighting and the combination of exterior neon-lit street shots and dark taxi interior shots highlighting Ponytail's death-like pallor are particularly suggestive.

We have not been encouraged by the cinematography and characterisation to invest too much concern in the Ponytail character at this point, but we are sufficiently interested in his fate to wonder whether he will make it to the nearest hospital. Typically deferring immediate satisfaction as to the outcome at this juncture, the film then cuts to the chase. Sergeant Lo, winded but vengeful, is pursuing one of the punks, who was waiting for him as he left the hot-pot restaurant and deliberately scratched the bodywork on his car. The punk is in fact leading Lo into a trap in a blue-lit deserted street between impersonal chrome office buildings. The wily Lo, guessing what is in store for him — the other three punks are standing ready with bats and improvised weapons — outwits them by approaching from an alternative direction behind them. Unfortunately the would-be hard man takes a pratfall, slipping on a banana skin in the pile of garbage under his feet in the alley-way, and knocking himself out cold, thereby placing himself at their mercy. The film eschews the beating he receives at their hands, and instead jump-cuts to the punks running out of the alley elated by their easy victory. They are just in time — third coincidence — to run headlong into the taxi driven by the dying Ponytail, careening out of control toward the pavement. It nearly hits them and they curse the anonymous driver loudly, as they run off, ironically unaware of the identity of its occupant and of the trouble that will accrue as a result. Not recognising their boss, they hurl standard curses in the general direction of the car driver, to the effect that they hope the driver will die, which of course is exactly what is happening. To's wicked sense of irony, cut loose from the moorings of conventional generic comedy, really flourishes in the noir context of this film. The musical soundtrack plays its part here by underscoring the chilly irony with an icy variation on the guitar theme, as the camera tracks in to the interior of the stationary taxi and comes to rest on the dead Ponytail slumped over the wheel.

Still 15 Waiting in alley to beat up Lo.

At this point the film cuts back to the alley and we see a rear view of Mike's patrol running to help Lo, who had obviously called for assistance. In fact Kat's patrol had reached the scene first. There is a close-up of the heavily cut and bruised Lo wearing an extensive head dressing, more likely a result of his heavy fall than of the beating administered by the gang of punks, one of the relatively low percentage of close-ups employed. Lo stoically refuses to register a complaint and rejects offers of an ambulance and hospitalisation.

Mike supports Lo's decision but then notices Lo's empty holster. The sharp-eyed Kat notices it too and is about to radio in a report on the missing gun when she is interrupted by Mike, who persuades her not to mention the fact, and offers to help Lo recover the 'stolen' gun before dawn. Kat is unhappy with this arrangement because it violates regulations and normal procedure, but Lo is anxious to avoid any blemish on his record since he is up for promotion next month. As his plea implies, a report on a missing gun would diminish his prospects, since it would suggest incompetence or neglect on his part. Despite the vagaries of life's banana skins, the policeman has to retain a positive and competent image, so honesty in this situation is clearly not the best policy from Lo's perspective. For the other officers however, now complicit in small-scale deceit, risking an official reprimand for the sake of Lo's promotion is not particularly appealing. Mike's persuasive persona and obvious authority win the day, although we see the two patrols bickering with each other in the background, using language reminiscent of the street punks in the previous scene.

The scene is a turning-point in the narrative, because a moral decision is made against a wonderfully rich background, in which Kat's and Mike's patrols wrangle with each other under the moody blue night lights, in sharp contrast to their respective sergeants standing perfectly immobile in the foreground of the frame. The acting is of the highest calibre with both Simon Yam and Maggie Shiu making excellent use of minimal movement and subtle facial expression, particularly the eyes. Mike stares reflectively ahead toward the camera, wondering what effect his loyal commitment to aid his brother officer will have on the night's events, and how the affair might be managed without negative fall-out. The scene as a whole is imbued with a feeling of moral equivocation and ambivalent attitudes, although we sense that Mike's over-riding loyalty to Lo might have its origins in his sense of indebtedness to Lo for a corresponding act of comradeship in the past. This is, however, only intuited in the interaction of the characters and no specific reference is made to the reason for Mike's spontaneous fraternal gesture toward a police officer from another unit. His decision to help Lo stands in stark contrast to the mutual suspicion and rivalry that appear to exist between the various police groups represented in the film.

The development: Rough tactics

The dissolve transition from the alley-way scene where we see Lo walking away with a bandaged head to Lo in his yellow paint-bespattered car heading away from Tsim Sha Tsui on Princess Margaret Road effectively marks the beginning of the next part of the film, though of course, as with most films, there is no clearly announced delineation between one part and the next. His mental state is evoked by low-angle shots of skyscrapers and disorientating images of the night-time city suffused in blue light. Tall buildings are seen to stick upward at odd angles into the bluish night, as Lo's car passes on its way to its destination. Lo, his face still streaked with blood (making a neat match with his paint-streaked car) puts a cigarette feverishly into his mouth and attempts to light the filter end — another nice little comic touch that is easy to miss. Since the beginning of 2007 smoking in many restaurants in Hong Kong is banned and as a social habit it has been widely discouraged. An unreconstructed macho, chain-smoker of the old school, Lo may well represent a dying breed. At any rate he is rarely seen in the film without the trademark Marlboro cigarette in mouth, incidentally the same brand as smoked by the triad kids. Lo's destination is a replica weapon shop — the shot presents us with a nondescript commercial centre probably located in either Yau Ma Tei or Mongkok — which one would normally expect to be shut at this time of night. Rousing the understandably disgruntled owner without apology, Lo persuades the latter to sell him a police standard plastic replica and, outside in his car once more, saws off the end of the barrel in order that the substitute weapon will fit his holster. To make it conform more closely to the requisite appearance, he carefully sprays it with black modelling paint. Satisfied with the results, he admires his handiwork and we are given a close-up of the finished article.

The film now cuts back to Mike's patrol in Tsim Sha Tsui patrolling the neon-lit streets, as the last of the shoppers head for home. The elongated figures of the PTU officers, shot from the rear, accentuate their dominating height, and they are symmetrically strung out across the frame, signifying a 'gang' or 'posse', as in old Hollywood westerns, heading for a showdown. The subsequent shot is brilliantly atmospheric. We hear the click-clack and shooting sounds of video games on the soundtrack, and then see blue-lit stairs and the steady plod of heavy combat boots descending the stairs. The depersonalised boots are soon connected with their owners as the remaining parts of the uniformed PTU officers come into camera view. However the macho impression given by the boots dominates the beginning of the scene, constituting an unforgettable establishing image. This is followed up by a wide shot of the video games parlour with its garish light and ubiquitous game machines, and we see a number of customers making a hasty exit, including those with psychotropic substances, who drop them on the floor and kick them under the nearest machine in order to avoid getting 'busted'. The canny customers — all of them youngsters — make for the exit, and we see one of Mike's subordinates removing the plug of the manager's close-circuit TV camera (with his omnipotent boot!) in order to ensure that nothing that happens in the interaction between the PTU officers and their intended 'targets' is on record. Mike and his men are looking for Ponytail's cousin whom they locate with some ease. He is surrounded by similarly aggressive punks to those of Ponytail's former entourage, and these play into Mike's hands by 'giving him lip'. Out-staring the hostile looks of the punks, Mike proceeds to ask their leader, Matt, about his cousin. He picks up Matt's inevitable packet of Marlboro and removes all but one of the cigarettes, suggesting that he could plant drugs and incriminate him, if Matt does not comply with his request for information. A medium close-up shot of a shaven-headed and rather truculent-looking acolyte of Matt is significant in the context of what happens next. Red-hued, to connote anger, conflict and blood, the image also gives us a meaningful close-up on the punk's dragon tattoo on his neck. Mike's experience tells him that this is the guy to intimidate, so he detains him having summarily dismissed the rest of the gang. Matt is now isolated and vulnerable, for all his cool bravado.

As the atmosphere becomes tense, To's instinctive sense of comedy comes into play once more. A curious youngster, who has remained at his video machine, turns his head to see what is going on, and one of Mike's subordinates directs him back to his game with the timely warning, 'Sei La!' (You're dying!) – but only in the context of his video game, of course. This is yet another example of To's visually sharp and linguistically succinct sense of humour, arising naturally from the dramatic situation. Visually speaking, this scene is full of the body language of ostension (pointing), which also helps to establish and assert the officers' authority. Pointing is, of course, a perfect visual metaphor for a *policier*/crime film, since one lead metaphorically, and even literally, points to another. In semiotic terms the action is indexical and refers to implications of meaning that cannot be fully grasped from the visual information of the immediate environment (mise-en-scène). Incidentally, this is as true for us, the audience, as it is for the fictional characters. Thinking ahead and assessing the situation and the presence of danger or of significant visual information are precisely the skills and habits that these PTU officers and Mike, as leader of the patrol, must hone. Equally, as intellectually curious cinema-goers we are required to interpret the signs conveyed to us by the film's codes and conventions. Thus when Mike points accusingly at the still surly but increasingly intimidated shaven-headed punk, and orders him to clean himself up by removing the dragon tattoo, the dominating body language, the configuration of the actors and the position of the camera leave us in no doubt that Mike's presence is commanding and that his will is iron. He backs up the threat of his accusatory finger, by slapping the punk hard across the face until he does as he is told. The latter eventually rubs the place on his neck raw and bloody.

Still 16 Mike in gaming arcade pointing at gang member.

The scene is inter-cut with shots of the interior of the taxi in Hanoi Road (supposedly) where Ponytail's mobile phone lies in a pool of blood on the floor. At this point Lo arrives on the scene just as his superior, Inspector Chan, and a forensic officer are investigating the gruesome murder. His first thought is that Ponytail might have been murdered with his own police-issue revolver, a worry that is comically allayed by the forensic officer merely nodding toward the huge knife sticking out of Ponytail's back, a statement of the grotesquely obvious. 'Was he stabbed to death? Any gunshot wound?' asks Lo, to which there is no rejoinder, only a brief withering look. The eerie street lighting and intermittent white flashes of the forensic photographer, together with the washed-out pallor of Ponytail's death mask face, make this a memorable scene.

Lo's vain superior is more concerned with the late-night mahjong game he is planning and which Lo himself is too beaten up to participate in. He wants to get the incident sorted out as soon as possible. 'What happened to you? You look like shit,' he remarks to Lo, as he slicks back his greasy hair. Instead of Lo, he invites the forensic specialist, Bill, to make up the mahjong foursome. At this point we get a repeat of the mobile phones routine with Bill's phone ringing first. Bill's young son is asking his dad about the pronunciation of a word. Bill asks his superior. 'Check the internet,' says his colleague dismissively, as if the internet is the source of all knowledge. The whimsy of this brief exchange, in itself entirely inessential for plot or character development, captures perfectly the casual cynicism of the 'let's just play' culture of Hong Kong. The mahjong game is more important than the homicide or Sergeant Lo's wounds or the son's homework. The PTU force's casual brutality is thus a microcosm of a wider social cynicism, and should not be viewed in isolation from societal attitudes that are often desensitised to and oblivious of the real world and the community.

The second call is on Ponytail's mobile phone from his persistent cousin, whose unwilling cooperation owes everything to Mike's intimidatory tactics. As before in the restaurant, Lo assumes it is his phone. It is at this point that the idea of answering it occurs to him, as the call might provide a lead. We see him struggle, albeit briefly, with vestiges of professional ethics, and then he reaches for the phone conveniently accessible to him in the open hatchback of the forensic investigator's car. This is followed by a superbly simple black-and-white close-up of Lo's white hand holding up the black Motorola against an all-dark background. Lo's temptation is not just an ethical one. Tampering with evidence would severely compound the problem of a missing weapon. Then the phone rings again and we look down on Lo from a crane shot position, as though invited to pass judgment on him from on high for his illicit actions. For of course he cannot resist the temptation to answer. Ponytail's cousin

Matt is perplexed when he hears Lo's unfamiliar voice, but Mike commandeers Matt's phone temporarily and moving away from earshot of Matt and his acolytes, has a brief conversation with his friend. 'Ponytail's boys may use my gun for revenge,' he confides in Mike, having informed him that the owner of his 'borrowed' mobile phone is dead. 'That would spell trouble,' acknowledges Mike.

There is no doubt that the contact between the two sergeants is important and thus Mike's rough tactics pay off, the end possibly justifying the means. Had Mike been less brutally insistent on getting a result, the train of events set in motion by Lo's appropriation of Ponytail's mobile phone would not have occurred. When we reflect on the sequence of interlocking events we realise that this scene is pivotal, because Mike has now become involved in the affair of the lost gun to the extent that psychologically he is hooked and shares Lo's obsession with the weapon. Perhaps more than his team members, he is experienced enough to appreciate the full extent of the calamity that would be visited upon Lo, if his lost weapon were indeed to be used in a revenge killing. The scene cuts from Mike and the resentful but subdued punk rubbing his wounded neck ruefully, to the CID car arriving on the scene. Inspector Chan's reaction to CID is distinctly unfavourable, and the hostile and suspicious Inspector Leigh Cheng soon manages to increase levels of animosity and rivalry between the respective units with her high-handed behaviour and (rightly) sceptical attitude toward her unprofessional male counterparts. We may note the relatively unsympathetic portrayal of this senior policewoman, which perhaps anticipates To's ambivalent depiction of the pushy female officer, Rebecca Fong, played by Kelly Chen, in *Breaking News*. However, it is important to see a degree of honesty on To's part in portraying this scenario of gender prejudice and mutual distrust in the police force. The British TV drama *Life on Mars* explores the fanciful idea of a contemporary policeman, by no means a New Age type of man, being transplanted back into the police force in the north of England in the early 1970s and being genuinely shocked by the sexist 'jokes' and patriarchal attitudes endemic to the police and the society of that era. To shows us in his depiction of Leigh Cheng, and of the far more sympathetically portrayed Sergeant Kat, that gender equality in the police force is a reality, despite the residual prejudices and stereotypes that still exist in Hong Kong, as elsewhere.

'Madam', as she is respectfully referred to by her 'boys' (who in their own way echo the behaviour of Ponytail's and Matt's willing acolytes) is immediately suspicious of Lo's behaviour. Not only does he look shifty, but he has obviously been involved in recent physical violence. The thinly disguised antipathy between the CID and the OCTB, as To represents it, is another cause of mutual suspicion. Leigh Cheng makes it clear that CID is taking over the case of Ponytail's violent death, and asks her boys to check on the inventory of his possessions. Forensic officer Bill is momentarily embarrassed by the disappearance of the mobile phone, and even the intervention of his superior, pressurising him to lie to the effect that they found no phone, does not help. He squirms uncomfortably under Madam's unforgiving stare, but is saved from further cross-examination by Lo, who suddenly appears with the mobile phone in question in a transparent plastic bag, rather lamely claiming that Bill 'dropped it'. We soon realise that Lo has switched phones for his own motives. Needless to say, this unconvincing explanation merely intensifies Madam's suspicion concerning Lo and his actions. The atmospheric scene closes with a medium-long shot of ambulance bearers carrying Ponytail's body away from the scene of the crash.

As in any film that depicts a number of protagonists or subjects, there is a considerable amount of cross-cutting between the principal interests of *PTU*. Up to this point the narration has tended to oscillate between the PTU group and the OCTB loner, Lo. Now the formal division of interest becomes more complex, since the CID trio has been introduced and the PTU group has sub-divided into two, Kat's patrol and Mike's patrol. From this point onward the perspective is four-fold, highlighting what Teo has persuasively described as the formal, abstract quality of To's film. At the same time it is fair to say that this consciously symmetrical construction is motivated by the film's themes and plot development, and cannot be dismissed as purely contrived and calculated. Appropriately there is a shift of focus to Kat's patrol investigating signs of systematic car break-ins in a street supposedly leading to Canton Road. Several car alarms are bleeping weakly and Kat calls for assistance from the regular police, since the matter appears to be too trivial for PTU involvement. On top of the mix of diegetic sounds of the car alarms comes the slow, sinister sound of an approach. Kat's group prepares to confront the possible miscreant, but all they see is a kid trundling round the corner on a BMX-type bicycle, nonchalantly licking an ice-cream. We see the kid at first from the point of view of the PTU officers, for whom he constitutes an anti-climax, but then the camera pulls away almost mockingly, underlining the incongruity of the situation. This is a further example of To's whimsical humour. The kid on the bicycle functions here, and again later in the film, as a kind of subversive 'joker' figure mocking the forces of law and order.

The film then cuts back to Mike's patrol further east across the other side of Nathan Road. To be precise, they are entering Cameron Lane, which is adjacent to the busier Cameron Road. Unlike the representation of Canton Road, Cameron Lane in this sequence plays itself. We know this because To shoots the scene to include a huge yellow Tom Lee sign, the distinctive music shop being located in this cul-de-sac. Given the tight restrictions on shooting in busier streets, To opts to mix authenticity with artifice in his representation of Tsim Sha Tsui. Indeed, the use of this and a few other genuine Tsim Sha Tsui locations enhance the film's successful blend of the real with the darkly surreal. Mike's group chase and run to ground an asthmatic informant in order to find out the whereabouts of Ponytail's boys.

As the long-haired thief runs headlong into an imaginary alley-way (imaginary in the real-life configuration of the back street, not in filmic terms!) a PTU officer steps out of the shadow and fells him with a vicious blow of his baton. The sadistic kicking of the informant that follows is possibly the low-point of the portrayal of the PTU, and the part of the film that was seen as most controversial and critical of police methods, partly because the young man stops breathing. Again, it is the experienced Mike who senses the danger of the man dying 'under police investigation', where his callow subordinates, especially the bespectacled officer, who literally 'gets his kicks' from the assault, seem oblivious to such a contingency. Mike himself performs artificial resuscitation on the potential informant, who dramatically comes back to life and sits bolt upright, just as the PTU team begin to worry that he has died. As he stands up and reaches for his inhaler a pack of stolen credit cards falls from his packet. Mike stamps his authority on the situation by placing his boot over the cards. Unsurprisingly, the informant is cooperative, and informs Mike that Ponytail's boys have a hang-out in an industrial building in nearby Minden Avenue. The younger rookie PTU officer, who has been acting as lookout while Mike's group extract the required information, has meanwhile been keeping the Station Orderly at arm's length to prevent him witnessing the scene in the alley. He has been detailed to join Mike's group, giving the pretext that he is bored by station work. The canny Mike guesses that the Orderly has been given the job of monitoring his activities. To's black humour is evident once again in the cynical way that Mike sees the informant on his way, exaggeratedly solicitous of his welfare. We note that he is allowed to hang on to his cache of credit cards. Again, this scene subtly and without sentiment or melodrama invites us to reflect on the question of ethical behaviour and on moral decisions in everyday police work.

Mike attempts to get rid of the unwelcome addition to his patrol, by telling the Orderly to join Kat's group. The atmospheric use of lighting and shadow under the yellow backdrop of the Tom Lee sign, as well as the use of low-angle medium long-shot, has the effect of 'blowing up' the modest and innocuous Cameron Lane and endowing it with almost sinister proportions. This is a good example of how Cheng Siu-keung's cinematography and To's direction promote the sense of hyper-reality alluded to in chapter 2. Teo refers to this quality of *PTU* as 'surreal'[2] but perhaps 'hyper-real' is more appropriate a word. The film's codes of realism remain strong throughout. Despite the 'nightmarish' nature of Lo's night, there is no conscious attempt to evoke the dream-like state or surreal style of mise-en-scène of, say, Richard Linklater's *Waking Life* — a self-consciously surreal contemporary film, if ever there was one. The shadows cast by the artificial light accentuate Mike's slow walk back to the rest of his team, after his terse conversation with the Orderly, slightly reminiscent of a western such as *The Wild Bunch* or *The Magnificent Seven*, films in which the group ethos and the configuration of the group in particular are paramount. Mike's colleagues are anxious to drop their self-appointed mission to help Lo find his gun. They have no desire to put their own jobs in jeopardy or run the risk of an official reprimand on Lo's account. 'You make your own decision,' says their laconic sergeant. As they walk away, followed by a reluctant Orderly, we are struck by the effectiveness of shots of the PTU officers' torsos and legs and note how even the textures of the uniforms are somehow made to look interesting and even cool. The shots of the patrol, strung out and not very cohesive in their grouping, as they turn back into Cameron Road, symbolically emphasise the sense of disunity that is emerging as a result of Mike's commitment to Lo.

We are then transported a few streets away, as the film cuts back to the indefatigable Lo making contact with one of his triad associates, Uncle Chung, played by veteran film director Wong Tin-lam, who plays memorable cameo roles in other To films such as *The Mission* and *Election I*. 'Hey, fat boy, what have you been up to?' asks the triad uncle, seeing the bloodied dressing around Lo's head and the bruises on his face, and shifting his own vast girth uncomfortably in the interior of his capacious people-carrier. Uncle Chung bears a message from his associate, Eyeball, whose gang has been blamed for the murder of Ponytail. Eyeball is seeking police protection, as he has heard on the grapevine that the grief-stricken Baldhead is seeking revenge and assuming that his rival is responsible. 'Eyeball never ordered the killing of Ponytail,' explains Chung. 'It's not my business,' says Lo, 'CID is following up the investigation now.' Right on cue Madam and her two lieutenants arrive on the scene and, having 'eyeballed' Lo accusingly, she orders her boys to rough up their own informant, whom they have dragged from a nearby pub. Lo watches as they apply a form of water torture to the unfortunate young man. 'We can't protect you for ever,' says the pitiless female inspector. Her intimidatory tactics echo those used by Mike's patrol (just as her bullying strong-arm boys are reminiscent of Ponytail's boys), and as with Mike's use of pressure to coerce the watching Matt, Madam's real target is not the young drug-sniffer himself, rather the watching Lo. The message conveyed to him is intended as a warning 'shot' that Madam is determined to get to the bottom of the affair. Distracted by the display put on for his benefit, Lo focuses his attention once more on Uncle Chung. 'Police protection is useless,' he says flatly, almost cynically, in subconscious harmony with Madam's cynical remark to her informer, but he agrees to meet Eyeball. He borrows a mobile phone battery from Chung. 'Don't forget to return it,' says Chung, providing another example of To's comical-ironic treatment of the theme of police-triad relations. As soon as Lo fits the battery in the phone it rings and he realises with a jolt of memory on answering, that he now has Ponytail's mobile phone, not his own. He throws it on top of the car dashboard, as though it was an explosive device, and then ruminates on the best course of action.

Complication and climax: Honour-bound

The climax of the film is perhaps something of a misnomer, since apart from the final shoot-out, the lead-up to the finale can best be described as a series of anti-climaxes, so that the end-game is all the more unexpected in its finality. If we share Lo's anxiety about the missing gun, and I am not sure that we really care all that much, we may be as alarmed as he is about the increasing complexities of the situation. More likely, the viewer is simply trying to keep abreast of events, not unlike the slightly bewildered PTU officers. They follow Mike, who is single-mindedly following up the thin lead he has obtained, which takes him to Minden Avenue, where Ponytail's 'boys' are said to be holed up. This is one of the classic scenes of the film, although in terms of plot, it is entirely gratuitous strictly speaking. Modern-day Minden Avenue no longer has industrial buildings — an indication of the gradual move up-market of the Tsim Sha Tsui area. Indeed, nearby Minden Row now sports a row of expensive restaurants in place of its former small clothing businesses and tenements. However one does not need to go far — Jordan, Yau Ma Tei, Hung Hom, for example — to see the type of streets and buildings that To wishes to bring to mind for this scene. Industrial buildings tend, in fact, to be more commonly found further afield, for example in areas like Mei Foo, Cheung Sha Wan and Kwun Tong. Perhaps the location of the spacious Milkyway Image headquarters in a former industrial building in Kwun Tong is an indication of To's predilection for these cinematically suggestive structures and the possibilities inherent in the sense of open space that they afford.

A soaring electric guitar reprise of the main theme motif with lots of echoing reverb accentuates the eerie, almost ethereal atmosphere of the scene. The PTU officers stop at the building seeing subdued lights emanating from an upper floor. Mike enters while his reluctant subordinates wait outside. The alternating interior and exterior shots emphasise the divisions between Mike and his men in terms of their perception of what constitutes duty. The slightly disorientating camera-work and accompanying music to this wordless sequence, as Mike advances slowly up the dark staircase, torch in hand, is particularly effective. We see Mike's progress from the exterior view of his colleagues in the disembodied movement of the torch beam against the sickly greenish surrounding colour scheme. As suspense is heightened, Mike becomes aware of a movement below and a second torch-light is visible. Anticipating attack, he turns, only to discover that the Orderly has joined him. One by one the other three members of his patrol follow suit, revealing the deeper underlying team spirit of the PTU group that prevails even in spite of their profound misgivings. The camera-work enhances the thematic idea of the sequence by presenting the officers on different levels with Mike at the top, symbolising his authority and the deep-rooted sense of hierarchy in the unit. As a complete and cohesive team they now approach the yellow door from which pale light is streaming. A forty-second tracking shot of the group waiting for the right moment to make their entrance audaciously racks up the suspense generated by the scene. Then they burst into the stripped-down interior to find three equally stripped-down young women, the eldest of whom picks up a feeble, impromptu weapon. 'Glasses' kicks her savagely in the chest, and, as she sprawls on the floor, the camera tilts downward revealing the imprint of his boot on the chest of her white tee-shirt. Ignoring her obvious pain, he motions to her to dust off the tell-tale mark. Self-preservation, not just among triads like Eyeball or Ponytail, is evidently uppermost in the minds of the characters of PTU. Naturally this entrance is anti-climactic. The scared women have no notion of the punks' whereabouts, after they were taken away earlier by Baldhead's men. Mike exhibits more sympathy than 'Glasses' and asks — apparently without any sense of irony — whether the women would like him to 'call the police', referring presumably to his common-or-garden counterparts in the regular force. The senior of the three 'comfort women', to use an infamous euphemism, takes a puff of her cigarette and shakes her head stoically. Like Lo she ignores her pain and is aware that complaining would only do more harm than good. Police assistance, like police protection, is clearly worthless in the situation and we are left with the haunting image of her closing her eyes to the mental and physical trauma of the evening's events.

Still 17 Ponytail's gang's hideout — girls.

Following this scene there is a wonderful cut and segue to a high-angle, long distance shot of the officers back on the street again. The camera captures the angular outline of the top of a building called the Golden Dragon Building (located in Jordan) bathed in eerie blue light, and then tilts slowly and continuously down to street level, where we see the patrol walking in formation, a far more cohesive and purposeful group than we had seen during the altercation on Cameron Road. The shot presents a strained and unnatural image of the otherwise deserted street, bluish-white in the middle where the light and movement are concentrated, darkening and shadowy at the edges. Sound provides the link to the human scale after this detached and distanced perspective. We hear Mike's attempt to contact Lo, which is unsuccessful. The immediate cut to the interior of Madam's CID car lets us know that the call has come through to

Lo's voice message box, and that his mobile is in the possession of Madam's boys. Mike's call alerts Madam to the fact that 'Ponytail's phone' actually belongs to someone else, and she is determined to trace the owner. Cutting back to Lo once more, we witness his comical reaction to more phone calls on Ponytail's mobile, which he answers in the hope they will provide a lead concerning the fate of his gun. The farce of the wrong phone is a motif that To seems to be able to repeat without recourse to the conventional licence of mainstream farce, probably because it is carefully authenticated and logically motivated by the tight plotting. Thus it never jars on the viewer, despite frequent iterations in the film. 'Ponytail, everyone says you're dead!' exclaims one caller, hastily terminating the connection. After a further two calls Lo's nerves are frayed to the limit, and he switches it off and throws it on the dashboard. However, on sober reflection he picks it up and calls Baldhead, who is predictably shocked to get a call from his dead son's mobile. After preliminary explanations they arrange to meet up, and Baldhead deviously promises to restore the gun to Lo, provided that the latter helps him take revenge on his rival, Eyeball.

Still 18 Back on the street — high-angle shot.

They meet up outside another nondescript industrial building and Lo follows Baldhead wordlessly inside the building flanked by the latter's toughs. As they ascend to an upper floor in the service lift we become aware of the tension, Baldhead mopping his brow constantly, Lo cocking his head to try and observe his intentions, and the bodyguards uneasy and antagonistic at having a cop in their midst. Baldhead's face is ominously accentuated by the fitful light and shadow of the lift grille. Once again To ensures that we feel the tension in the air by prolonging the lift's ascent virtually to real time. He reveals himself here, as in other films, to be a great filmmaker in his close observation of the behaviour of small male groups working under stress and strain. What follows is yet another of the scenic *tours de force*, in which this film is so remarkably rich. Escorted by Baldhead's minions through a storage area, Lo suddenly comes into a large bare space with a few bicycles parked incongruously against the far wall. The only other objects in the room are four cages which appear to contain animals. The camera tilts up to reveal the petrified face of one of Ponytail's punks, now shaven-headed and naked and bent double, looking out through the bars of the cage. Panning across to the other cages in the empty space we get a vision of sheer savagery.

Yet To refuses to invite us to empathise with these 'victims', representing the scene in grotesque Hieronymus Bosch–like visual style. The contrast between the former swaggering, fashionable street-punks who had preyed on the hapless and defenceless Lo with the caged sub-humans of the scene is striking. Truly pride came before their fall and a terrible poetic justice, albeit coincidental, has been meted out to Lo's aggressors. 'Why are you looking for the punks,' Baldhead suddenly asks. 'Don't play with me. You know why,' rejoins Lo gamely. In fact Baldhead does not know, but soon works out how he can manipulate the police sergeant by pretending to have his gun. 'I know you have my son's mobile. I know Eyeball is your friend, right?' he asserts, to which Lo replies 'I'm not involved. I'm only trying to find my gun. I can't handle this.' But of course, willy-nilly, Lo is involved and has no choice but to 'handle it'. When

Baldhead proposes a deal, whereby Lo gets his gun back at the price of luring Eyeball into a trap, Lo protests, 'You want me dead? I'm a cop!' The mention of death sends Baldhead into a rage and he picks up a hammer and smashes it against the bars of the cage containing one of the unfortunate punks. 'Why did my son have to die, why not you?' he rants in his paternal anguish.

Lighting up what seems to be his hundredth cigarette of the night to steady his skittish nerves, Lo walks away, knowing he has little choice but to accept Baldhead's compromising deal. Believing him to have the gun, Lo recognises that Baldhead holds all the aces. As he leaves the building a fine drizzle is falling slantwise, its gossamer texture strangely beautiful in the silvery light. In its subtle way the sudden rain reminds us symbolically that we really do not know what is going to happen from one moment to the next. Lo's search appears no closer to the desired outcome, but the rain seems to provide an interlude and a feeling of respite, quite apart from the sense of physical relief that light rain brings on hot summer Hong Kong nights. At this point we get a jump cut to the PTU patrol running round the corner of Carnarvon Road in Tsim Sha Tsui, followed by the image of the implacable Inspector Leigh Cheng grimly watching the rain fall from the interior of her car while one of her lackeys is getting wet making his inquiries about Lo's phone. The rain is a linking motif here inasmuch as it falls on each of the four subjects, although of course two of them can shelter in cars. As we cut back to Mike's patrol, the camera tilts to reveal the officers running harder now to get 'protection' from the increasingly heavy rain. In Carnarvon Road the PTU patrol rendezvous with the supply truck distributing raingear. Lo calls Mike and explains that the punks had no obvious motive for revenge by picking up his gun, because when they beat him up they had no idea Ponytail had been murdered. They arrange to meet at the PTU's regular refreshment locale, the 'Bing Sat' café. Immediately we cut back to a vindictive-looking Madam, receiving the news from her subaltern that 'Ponytail's mobile phone' in fact belongs to Lo Sa. Clearly she is out to get him. Next there is a brief shot of Lo calling the credulous Eyeball to make arrangements to take him in for 'police protection', and thereby indicating to the viewer that he has decided to play ball with Baldhead.

Still 19 PTU officers running round the corner in the rain.

Lo drives up and parks his conspicuous yellow-and-blue-striped car outside the 'Bing Sat', and, ignoring the protestation of the manager that they are closed, marches directly upstairs to find Mike. We are treated to a great overhead shot of the ceiling fan turning inexorably, suggesting perhaps that the police officers are simply going round aimlessly in circles, and then Lo makes contact with Mike under the disapproving eyes of his team members. Sergeant Kat's group arrives, and she in turn gives the table where Mike and Lo are ensconced in *sotto voce* discussion a searching, censorious gaze. 'Don't patrol Canton Road at 4 a.m.,' pleads Lo. 'Can you sign in at 4.30 instead?' Kat comes over and enquires trenchantly of Lo, 'Found your gun yet?' Receiving no reply she returns to her team, orders a lemon coffee and proceeds to stare hard at her two conspiratorial male colleagues. 'It's 2 a.m. already. Everything will be over by 4,' says Lo. 'Help me, Ah-Jin.'

Mike is honour bound by the *jianghu* code to help Ah-Sa, as the symbolism of the pair's nicknames reveals. Ah-Sa ('Sarge', but also his full name, Lo Sa) and Ah-Jin (Ho Man-jin, Mike's Cantonese name) are literally complementary. The Cantonese morphemes 'Sa' and 'Jin' when juxtaposed give 'Sergeant', or '*Sa-jin*', clearly no coincidence in the choice of names for the screenplay. In fact, it does not matter if we miss it. In *PTU*'s deliberately understated way the inter-relationship of Mike and Lo is hinted at, rather than spelled out for us in the over-written screenplay of a typical police film concerned with partners and buddies. If this constitutes the crime of plot and character 'under-development', To and screenwriters Yau Nai-hoi and Au Kin-yee are gloriously guilty of it. But film enthusiasts who hate to have their intelligence insulted by formulaic over-elaboration will laud them for their transgression.

Just when Lo glimpses a happy outcome, or at least the successful recovery of his weapon, the relentless Madam appears at the top of the stairs with her boys, effecting a dramatically authoritative entrance. 'Good thing your car was easy to spot,' she remarks caustically to the apparently cornered Lo Sa. 'Why do you have Ponytail's phone?' Faking a nonchalant smile, Lo tries to wriggle out of the situation by claiming he took the mobile phone, mistaking it for his own. 'Eyeball has called you,' Madam responds accusingly. Knowing he cannot bluff his way out, Lo makes a dash for the emergency exit, demonstrating unexpected quickness off the mark for a car-bound chain-smoker! Significantly Kat steps aside obligingly, despite the fact that she was well placed to block his escape or trip him up. Not a single member of the PTU team lifts a finger to help the CID plain-clothes boys, making it quite clear to Madam where their loyalties lie — not with Lo, but with each other. Mike 'wears the uniform' and is one of their own, never mind his unorthodox actions. Madam tries to give the PTU team 'the third degree' but they studiously ignore her, finding their bowls of noodles utterly absorbing. Not a single eye meets hers, and when her underlings return empty-handed, she threatens in her undisguised frustration, 'If anything happens to Lo, you'll *all* be held responsible.' As she departs, the team, Mike and Kat included, continue eating and drinking calmly, as if they had not witnessed the scene at all.

The dénouement — 'Uncoiling the spring'

The French term *le dénouement*, as used to signify resolution in dramatic structure, employs the metaphor of unravelling tangled threads. This metaphor is appropriate enough since the plot-lines have certainly been complex and Baldhead, Lo and even Mike have woven tangled webs in order to deceive others and obfuscate their motives. In the opening chapter, however, I referred to French dramatist Anouilh's use of the idea of a coiled spring uncoiling with mechanical inevitability to produce the tragic ending, and this trope is also relevant in my view to the film's sense of closure. As we shall see, a generically tragic outcome is not quite the case with *PTU*'s resolution, since this film and its companion piece, *Breaking News*, have the most satisfying of To's endings from the perspective of law enforcement. Nevertheless, the last part of the film is tense, exciting and dark in the way it arranges the chain of events, leading inexorably forward to the collision of various forces at their fate-appointed hour. This is very much redolent of classical tragedy, in which so-called 'unities' of subject, time and location are conventionally observed. The events of *PTU* avoid extraneous characters and concentrate on those who participate in the final showdown. The film's narrative action is, as we have seen, compressed within an eight-hour, overnight period of time on the night of 14 September and early morning of 15 September. Lastly, Tsim Sha Tsui, notionally at least, functions as the concentrated locus of dramatic action. The German film critic Ekkehard Knörer who described the film as 'Ein Meisterwek der Konzentration' (a masterpiece of concentration)[3] clearly knew what he was talking about. To admits to re-considering the ending, prompted by a suggestion from the curator of the New York Film Festival, in order to make it less tidy. However his original instincts were, I think, entirely vindicated by the result.

Most of the remaining events of the movie are supposed to be concentrated in Canton Road, by the waterfront in Tsim Sha Tsui, although poetic licence must be exercised, since the Hong Kong–based filmgoer knows that this Canton Road is a nostalgic recreation of To's youth. Contemporary Canton Road, very much part of an ultra-modern, highly developed Hong Kong waterfront, no longer resembles this quiet, dark, open stretch with cars parked at the kerb-side. This explains why the filmmakers chose Ap Lei Chau on the less developed south side of Hong Kong Island to stand in for Canton Road. We see a small nerdy fellow, reminiscent of the nervous-looking assassin in the hot-pot restaurant, minus the long curly hair, signalling to an approaching boat. The next shot is from the perspective of the unseen occupant of the boat, the rocking of the camera and the reflections of the light on the water giving the impression that we, the viewers, are swaying with the motion of the boat, as it approaches the choppy water close to the jetty. The lookout runs round the corner to telephone his on-shore contacts and runs into Lo heading for the same phone, intent on finalising the tricky arrangements for Eyeball and Baldhead to encounter each other, unbeknown to the former. Not wanting any more calls or mobile phone usage to be traced by his nemesis, the zealous Inspector Leigh Cheng, Lo opts for the phone booth — at exactly the same time as the nerdy fellow. For a comical moment the two are frozen to the spot, uncertain who should have priority. 'Moron,' says Lo under his breath, as the other guy whips out a mobile phone to resolve the impasse.

Lo makes his call from the booth, and returns to his car when he is struck by the possibility of duplicity on Baldhead's part, so he goes back to make a second call, only to bump into the same fellow intent on using the phone booth once again. The repetitive visual slapstick of the scene is all the funnier for being played down, as the sort of farcical situation that often materialises in real life. Lo even gives the other guy, who has exhausted his supply of coins, change for his call, unaware that he is a lookout for a criminal gang (as we are too, although we have the nagging suspicion that we have seen him before). He refuses the proffered note in return and returns to his car. Lo's generous behaviour towards the other caller is extremely ironic given their subsequent interaction, but as the film tells us, we really do not know what tricks life will play on us. The next phone call is a mobile call from Madam's drug-dependent informer, telling her that Baldhead will 'make his move tonight', so Madam and her boys drive to Baldhead's headquarters and determine to tail him.

The film cuts first to the eastern part of Tsim Sha Tsui where Mike is trying to avoid going anywhere near Canton Road in compliance with Lo's request. The Orderly helpfully reminds him that they are supposed to sign in at Canton Road very shortly according to the schedule, and expresses surprise at Mike's poor sense of direction. Another swift cut takes us back to Canton Road, where once again the whirring sound of the boy's bicycle causes Kat's group to turn in anticipation of danger. Unsure of the connection between the inexplicable shattering of car windows and the presence of this *sei jai bao* (Cantonese for 'little sod'), Kat's group stays and watches, while the boy pedals off underneath a gigantic advertising hoarding, on which is displayed a vastly extended bikini-clad woman. The copy on the advertisement exhorts us to join the captioned health and beauty club, the relaxed and healthy message of the poster standing in stark but ironic juxtaposition to the events that follow. Kat remains alert, and her eyes narrow, as the camera comes toward her in medium close-up.

Still 20 Billboard and gangsters.

Waiting impatiently once more for his new friend to finish his third attempt to get through, Lo curses under his breath. The offending caller apologises courteously and Lo makes his third call — a vain attempt to convince Baldhead that his rival had nothing to do with the killing of his son. One way of reading the startling similarity of the other caller in physical terms to Ponytail's killer is that the murder was a distraction, designed as a smoke-screen to keep the police busy while the mainland gang make a clean get-away. Such a speculative reading makes the phone conversations and interaction between Lo and the lookout even more ironic, and also provides a kind of poetic justice in the way the character gets his come-uppance. Meanwhile Baldhead is adamant, that only by producing Eyeball can Lo recover his gun. 'Eyeball is mine,' snarls Baldhead, 'You'll get your gun back. Nothing will matter after tonight.' As it turns out his predictions prove to be entirely accurate, but a worried Lo replies lamely, 'You'd better keep your promise.' We then cut back to Madam and her boys observing Baldhead's departure with the instructions to his mystified acolytes that he is not to be followed, again ironic in view of Madam's terse command to her driver, 'Follow him.'

If some of the inter-cutting between characters and locations up to this point of the film was possibly intended to be synchronous, the synchronicity of the next scenes is beyond doubt and is signified by means of a countdown to 4 a.m. with only minutes to go. The next cut takes us back to Mike's patrol, now showing signs of impatience about their dereliction of duty. 'Brother Mike,' says the Orderly, 'time to sign in at Canton Road. It's nearly 4 a.m.' Mike tries to use diversionary tactics to delay them further and suggests signing in retroactively, but the Orderly insists. 'Don't forget you're not an officer,' declares Mike, pulling rank. 'What shall I say to the superintendent?' asks the frustrated Orderly, 'that Lo asked you to skip Canton Road?' Mike rejoins coolly, 'Tell him anything you like!' But the Orderly appeals to his conscience, 'Anyone wearing the uniform is one of our own. We're on the same team,' implying both that his sense of team solidarity prevents him from telling tales, and simultaneously that Mike's devious behaviour is dishonouring the PTU uniform. 'You know this isn't right,' he persists, 'you know we'll all get into trouble for this.' Mike just stares back impassively and we are left wondering how the deadlock will be resolved.

Still 21 Jay Chou concert poster — street scene.

The stage is set for the film's remarkable finale. First we see Kat's patrol searching for more clues to explain the sequence of car alarms that appears to indicate criminal activity in the area. Shifting from under another advertising hoarding publicising a forthcoming Jay Chou concert, they move back to their original position at the sea-end of the street and here they lie patiently in wait in the shadows of parked vehicles to catch those responsible. As it transpires, this is a fortuitously advantageous location for the unanticipated shoot-out. When it comes it is swift and violent, but the most impressive aspect of the mise-en-scène is the brilliant integration of the plot strands into one concise and masterly conclusion. Kat's team witness the junior thief on the bicycle approach a car with the intention of burgling the contents. Then Lo hears the sound of a car approaching. Eyeball arrives first, gets out of his car and walks toward the worried Lo, still standing by the phone booth. Immediately afterwards Baldhead arrives on the scene and 'smells a rat'. 'Screw you, Lo!' he yells. Madam pulls up in her car, close to where Lo is standing, and glares at him with a look of vindictive triumph. Simultaneously the mainland robbers arrive by taxi, lulled into a false sense of security by the phone call. Their astonishment when they realise they have company provides another of the great darkly comical moments of the film. Medium close-ups on each of the participants in the coming confrontation emphasise their growing realisation of a do-or-die conflict. The ensuing gun-fight is filmed partly in slow motion, giving an oddly B-movie western feel to the close-range shoot-out between Baldhead and Eyeball, in which they shoot each other to death — inexpertly. By contrast the precision shooting of the two PTU patrols, firing from the steady positions instilled into them by years of rigorous training, is more effective. The gangsters, exposed to view like the woman in the giant advertisement above their heads, are unprepared, their bulky machine weapons concealed in leather cases. By the time they are capable of returning fire, they are already riddled with accurately aimed bullets and spurting blood from multiple wounds.

Two superb pieces of imagery enhance the quality of this finale. The first is the arrival of Mike's group running round the corner of the street, obviously united once more in their commitment to their duty.

The second is the comical, rather pathetic sight of Lo with his hands to his ears, trying to block out the sound and vision of the nightmare scenario that has erupted before his eyes. When the lookout attempts to intervene, Lo snaps out of his traumatised state and goes for his gun — the plastic replica — which he drops in impotent rage before making a run for it. The lookout immediately sets off in vengeful pursuit. At the same time Madam attempts to shoot from the car, but drops her gun, making her a sitting target. Cowering inside the car to avoid detection, Madam's life is saved by Lo, whose unsuspected identity as a police officer attracts the ire of his former 'phone-box mate'. However this is not before Madam endures moments of sheer terror as the gangster's weapon is framed against the misted car-window. Lo runs into the self-same alley where he was beaten up earlier, slips on the same banana-skin, and, as his assailant takes aim to shoot, Lo flails instinctively for support and feels a weapon mysteriously in his grasp. His missing gun, now miraculously restored, does not fail him and the gangster falls dead, a bullet in his forehead.

Still 22 Lo screaming with his hands to his head.

By the time Lo returns to the scene of the shoot-out, everything is over and the clean-up operation — in more senses than one — is beginning. Passing the badly shaken Inspector Cheng, Lo grins and hold his gun up with aplomb. Madam has the grace to say sorry to Lo and he responds in a spirit of reconciliation. He sees her gun lying on the ground, an ironic parallel to the temporary loss of his own weapon. 'Fire a couple of shots, Madam, it'll look good in your report,' he advises her. She does as he suggests, the dull report of her two shots sounding oddly anti-climactic after the intensity of the fire-fight. Lo triumphantly shows his recovered weapon to the relieved Mike Ho, chortling over the absurdity and pointlessness of most of the night's exertions. All's well that ends well, as the three groups file their highly fictitious radio reports with headquarters and call for an ambulance to pick up the dead gangsters. Inadvertently and fortuitously the combined forces of the PTU, CID and OCTB have avenged the loss of one of their own in the North Point bank robbery, eliminated the unscrupulous mainland gang, engineered the mutual destruction of two of the city's most powerful triad bosses, and covered their respective (and rival) police units in shared glory. Not a bad end to a night's work that began on such an inauspicious note. The film closes with the unforgettable image of the kid on his bicycle pedalling toward the camera. Now that the police cars and the PTU truck have left the scene, the stage is his alone, and he can continue with his nocturnal activities with no sign of dawn's approach. The camera fades to black as the twinkling pin-points of light recede. The night may 'have a thousand eyes', but none are trained on him, and the friendly darkness will abet his petty larceny. Reflecting on the film's tense and unexpected resolution, we realise that To has conjured up both a compromised and unsentimental ending that oscillates between the upbeat and the downbeat. How do we assess or evaluate such a film?

Still 23 Back in the PTU van after the shoot-out.

4

The Coda: What's the Story? — Morning Glory!

Whatever happened to all the heroes?
All the Shakespearos?
They watched their Rome burn
No more heroes any more
No more heroes any more
— The Stranglers, from the 1977 song 'No More Heroes'

'*PTU* is a refreshing subversion of an entire Hong Kong genre of films that seek easy heroism in rogue cops out for justice and sharply dressed gangsters who live by the codes. In *PTU* there is no code and less justice. A bit like real life.'
— Bryan Walsh, *Time Asia*, 12 May 2003

'To's idiosyncrasy arises from a constant urge to renew himself not only to produce work that is different from the classical norms of the Hong Kong cinema (and its inter-textual references to Hollywood and Japanese cinemas) but from his own norms ...'
— Stephen Teo, *Director in Action — Johnnie To and the Hong Kong Action Film*, 209

'The Blue Curtain': Concealing, revealing

The brief coda of the film following the decisive shoot-out is easy to overlook, since the tension has been entirely dissipated by the film's explosive set-piece finale. However, like everything else about *PTU*, it is rewarding to examine in some detail. As Lo returns from his redemption in the alley, reports are being radioed back to headquarters. The Orderly informs his PTU superintendent merely that there was 'a fire situation' in Canton Road, that everything is under control, that there are six Chinese male casualties, and that all the officers are fine. Significantly, he makes no mention of Mike's unorthodox behaviour. An ambulance is also called to the scene. From the rear of the PTU truck that has arrived to pick up the night patrol, Mike radios in his own report: 'PTU B2 Unit, Police Sergeant Mike Ho reporting. We were patrolling Canton Road ...' he begins untruthfully. Sergeant Lo Sa of the Anti Crime Division B begins his narrative: 'I was off-duty and was passing Canton Road ...' This is not in any respect a version of events that the audience will recognise, of course, but it dovetails neatly with the PTU report of events. As for Inspector Leigh Cheng, her falsehood is simply the one suggested to her by Lo: 'I backed up my colleagues and fired two shots ...' Lo goes on to present a slightly revised, but of course entirely credible, account of the shooting of his pursuer: 'During the gunfight a gunman fled. I pursued him into a back alley. When the gunman pointed his gun at me, I was forced to fire back twice.' Since the 'good guys' have prevailed, it seems churlish to quibble about these blatant rearrangements of the actual facts we have been privy to. In any case none of the officers appears at all uncomfortable with this neatly revisionist interpretation of events. Why should we worry, since poetic justice and the interests of the law-abiding majority have been served by the satisfactory outcome? Presumably the officers will be highly commended by their superiors and lionised by the Hong Kong press on the morrow, thus emphasising the success of the authorities in tackling criminals within the SAR as well as predatory gangs from across the border. From the director's and screenwriters' perspectives, however, revealing the convenient lies of the representatives of law and order seems to be significant, otherwise care would not have been taken to add such a specifically detailed coda to the film's grand finale.

Are To and his collaborators inviting us to lament the rottenness and blinkered self-interest endemic to the police force, as in Scorsese's dark view of the custodians of public safety in *The Departed*? (Let's remember that natural justice in the end of Scorsese's version has to be administered by the disillusioned, maverick ex-cop played by Mark Wahlberg). To's film, however, is very different in its implications. We neither condemn nor condone the police officers' instinctive response to the situation, which prompts them to be economical with the truth. Their superiors prefer neat endings, and so does the public at large – just as cinema-goers like neat endings too (which of course is what To has given us with a strong dash of ironic whimsy). The inquest into the Tsui Po-ko case, just like other official inquests and enquiries into police action in other countries, reveals the marked tendency on behalf of the authorities to avoid opening cans of unwholesome worms. We are all complicit in the fabrications and half-truths that are regularly purveyed in most modern societies. For those of us who read more deeply about what actually occurred, the utterly unconvincing official narrative intended to 'explain' the events of 11 September 2001 are a case in point. In order to achieve closure and construct a more palatable narrative that reassures society and enhances people's faith in law enforcement, it is essential that a recognisable heroic narrative be extrapolated from the rather amorphous real events, which are in any case conveniently ephemeral and usually unrecorded or sketchily recorded. In this film Johnnie To has relentlessly forced us to acknowledge our complicity in society's dirty, nocturnal compromises. After all, they are our police force and their methods reflect our society's obsession with convenient grand narrative and the basic human craving for myths and heroes.

Yet we know — as postmodern deconstructionist theory has argued and many writers and filmmakers have reminded us — that such constructions of 'truth' rely on shared, willing self-delusion, that whatever 'truth' we can establish is often relative rather than absolute. As the old punk song by the Stranglers observed, after Leon Trotsky and Pancho Villa there are 'no more heroes any more — no more Shakespearos'. To grew up in the era of Hong Kong's economic boom and his work often reflects the spirit of optimism, or at least the view that one can succeed by one's own efforts. At the same time he was part of a generation that, like its own heroes such as Jean-Luc Godard, had begun to question establishment values and 'grand narratives', to use Lyotard's influential formulation. In the last fifty years we have seen a plethora of books and films driven by a profound scepticism toward official rhetoric and doctrine, not only in the West but also in Asia. In a city as influenced as Hong Kong has been by Western values, fashions and films, it would be surprising if a talented and independent-minded director like To were not at some level affected by the currents of contemporary thought. In *PTU* his scepticism is fused with the spirit of fatalism that is pervasive in his recent output. However, *PTU* also marks the beginning of a more socially and politically critical phase in his filmmaking. For example, the dark conclusion of his 2005/6 two-part blockbuster *Election* expresses in wonderfully restrained allegory his and many Hongkongers' misgivings about the electoral process in Hong Kong and about behind-the-scene mainland interference, as well as collusion with reactionary vested-interest groups.

In interview (see Appendix) To talks about the idea of covering the city with 'an invisible Blue Curtain'. This metaphor initially suggests the idea of outnumbering and overwhelming the lawless or dangerous elements that threaten public safety. It brings to mind the strikingly similar British English concept of the police force as 'the thin blue line' standing between law and order and total anarchy. The metaphor To uses may owe something to the Hong Kong Police Force's British colonial antecedents, and perhaps also to the title of Errol Morris's 1978 documentary essay film. The 'Blue Curtain' phenomenon is very much in evidence in the ending of *PTU* as the combined fire-power of the PTU officers in their blue berets and blue rain-capes eliminates the threat posed by the gangsters. The CID representatives (Madam and her boys) and the maladroit Sergeant Lo are simply out of their depth, as Madam's inept handling of her weapon and Lo's horrified reaction reveal. Thus the film is ultimately a kind of ambivalent homage to the Police Tactical Unit, but pulls no punches about demonstrating the full range of their punches. In the Cantonese-language DVD interview, among many interesting observations, To has a few things to say about his ambivalent approach. One of his most revelatory, albeit coy, comments is this one:

> Viewers from overseas and from Hong Kong have asked me if cops really do what is shown in the movie. I don't want to say. Things happen in life. It is not a creation of my movie. If you read the paper or watch the news, you know what goes on. Criminals will not admit on their own that they have committed a crime. Something has to happen in between to make them admit their guilt. I don't want to focus on the violence. Some will think that it is just the right thing to do, while some will think it wrong. For the purposes of my movie it doesn't matter. It is just a story point. What I wanted to show was how policeman protect themselves and each other. Protecting each other is a strong ethic in the police force, because a policeman is only one instant away from being in the same situation as a criminal ... Day in and day out, the police face things that are beyond reason. They deal mostly with the abnormal and unusual.[1]

The PTU patrol certainly deals with the abnormal situation that materialises in Canton Road, even if the officers do not manage to solve the case of the cheeky young thief on the bicycle. Moreover, the group exact fitting revenge for the death of the colleague some of them had spoken so disrespectfully about on hearing the news of the heist by the mainland gang at the opening of the film. Ironically this revenge is *de facto* and entirely unwitting. Nevertheless, there is a sense of retribution for all such violations of Hong Kong's civil society by mainland gangs, which was becoming increasingly common in the 1990s. Allegorically speaking, one can read it as Hong Kong's desire for revenge against all of the mainland's incursions and infringements on its territory and property. Naturally To's reference to the idea of a 'Blue Curtain' constitutes a dual, as opposed to a single-meaning, metaphor. A curtain's principal function is to conceal, and this is precisely what happens in the film's closure. The Blue Curtain, designed to protect police interests, closes on the night's events. What has gone on under cover of night is obscured and obfuscated by the official version being purveyed by the winners of the fire-fight. The public does not need to know and maybe does not want to know. The police control the narrative. Their form of recount of events is no more than a homogenised, manipulated semi-fiction designed to protect the police as a body, and as such represents just another social discourse, not the essence of objective truth. In revealing the police report as one of many discourses (of which the film itself is also merely one), containing elements of a relative truth but also deliberate fictions and distortions of fact, To and his screenwriters make us aware of the compromises and ethical dilemmas involved in police work.

As in many of To's best films his characters are compromised and flawed, which is of course what makes them interesting. The cool-headedness of the PTU unit under fire is indisputable. They may not be heroes in the absolute Superman sense of super-heroism, but they do not flinch. Their discipline and *esprit de corps* see them through, and they are in their own relative way heroic. In any case they do not seek hero status, just survival, career opportunity and as normal a life as possible in the abnormal circumstances in which they find themselves. What is clear is that they can no longer be the heroes they once were in films like *Lifeline*. To's directorial evolution in his choice of leading man from recognised hero (Lau Ching-wan) to indeterminate hero-villain (Simon Yam) is highly significant in this respect. It is indicative of the evolution of his style and perspective. The 'heroism' of the PTU group is to a large extent the product of their arduous training routines, and the film's protagonists can no longer be construed as paragons of civic virtue in the Lau Ching-wan mould. Indeed some commentators, Stephen Teo included, have seen the absence of Lau Ching-wan in To's later oeuvre as a loss, precisely because he exudes a recognisable and unequivocal quality of Hong Kong heroism. Such criticism seems to miss the point that To no longer wants to make the same type of movie after *The Mission* as he did before — at least not in the context of his 'exercises' category.

In any event, neither Lau, nor his namesake Andy from *Fulltime Killer* and *Running Out of Time*, would convey the quality of indeterminacy that a film such as *PTU* requires. As discussed in earlier chapters, To's direction and Chung's camera-work aim at downplaying empathy with the subjects, and even in the shoot-out we remain relatively distanced from them. The whimsically laconic Lam Suet as bumbling Sergeant Lo is no suave, charismatic Alain Delon. The exceptionally talented Simon Yam has positive qualities and established cinematic charisma, but his portrayal of Ho is deliberately distanced throughout the film. Rather as Jean-Pierre Melville did when Delon acted in his films, To finds a way of integrating the star perfectly into his work, be it Lau Ching-wan, Tony Leung or Simon Yam, in such a way that the film does not revolve around him. We may recall that Melville always used a strong, all-round cast in films like *Le Samouraï*, *Le Cercle Rouge* and *Un Flic*, films in which Delon's performance is counter-balanced by equally impressive contributions from the other actors. To's tendency to prefer ensemble actors, especially in this film, *The Mission* and *Exiled*, is therefore typical of his disregard for the pervasive Hong Kong idol culture. Even box-office names such as Tony Leung Ka-fai, Andy Lau and Lau Ching-wan are cast in his films for their qualities as actors, not for their star status. A distinct dearth of Ekins, Edisons, Jays, Gillians and Charlenes (all Hong Kong pop/cinema idols) is what we have come to expect from To's serious films and *PTU* takes this characteristic approach to the very limits of anti-chic. In its own way, of course, the film's zoom shots of the PTU officers firing in battle formation with Simon Yam crouching at the centre of the image provide brief moments of cinematic allure, the sort that is more associated with the hard-bitten, flawed Clint Eastwood type of 'hero', rather than the conventionally fresh-faced starlet of the Hong Kong star system. This phenomenon is related closely to the philosophy of To, which has nothing to do with Hong Kong's crassly commercialistic stereotype and everything to do with its underlying spirit of fatalism and endurance.

Still 24 Mike and colleagues not flinching under fire.

To neglects to pay homage to the tried and trusted glamour principles pervading the Hong Kong film industry, which dictate that the film is simply a vehicle for the movie/pop star. In films like *PTU, Breaking News* and *Election* he commits brazen heresy in respect of Hong Kong's widely admired and now venerable 'heroic bloodshed' genre. Memorably apostrophised as 'ballistic ballet' or 'bullet 'n brotherhood' movies by Bey Logan, the genre reached its apogee around the time of the Tiananmen Square Massacre, which perhaps reflected in an indirect way the idea of heroic self-sacrifice and a pathos-infused loyalty that transcends triad codes. The gangster chic component of the genre, influenced both by the Hollywood tradition and French *policiers*, was given a cool Asian twist, as epitomised by Chow Yun-fat in *A Better Tomorrow*. Inevitably nearly all of Hong Kong's film directors owe something to the heroic bloodshed genre, but the stylised gun battles and contrived heroism of the genre served to construct their own myths about Hong Kong, myths that do not bear harsh scrutiny. Bryan Walsh perceptively commented on the deconstructive aspect of *PTU* in his *Time Asia* review quoted above, referring to To's approach as 'subversive'.[2] It is, for example, noteworthy that the only sharply dressed characters in To's film are the PTU officers themselves, whereas the gangsters are signally un-chic. To's very un–Hong Kong–like scepticism about authoritative discourses, though implicit, is clearly deconstructive in spirit (for 'deconstructive', people in the business of cinema, and the business of government, tend to read 'destructive').

Arguably, though, it was high time Hong Kong stopped viewing its 'heroic bloodshed' films nostalgically through the rose-tinted spectacles of admirers like Quentin Tarantino. The genre did Hong Kong proud in the late 1980s and 90s and produced such classics as John Woo's *A Better Tomorrow* (1986), *The Killer* (1989), *Bullet in the Head* (1990) and *Hard Boiled* (1992), as well as Ringo Lam's *City on Fire* (1987) and *Full Contact* (1992). For contemporary 'action' directors these films are hard acts to follow, and in any case times have changed. One important difference between the 'heroic bloodshed' era and today's world is that Hong Kong is now a postcolonial society, which complicates the relatively straightforward state of affairs in the depiction of the city in those earlier films. To's rather un-heroic treatment of his characters is un-melodramatic and un-sentimental in accordance with the un-heroic times in which we live, whereas heroic bloodshed movies tended to be dynamically gory but also heavily sentimentalised in their presentation of the sympathetic protagonists. To's melodramatic strain was evident in his Chow Yun-fat vehicle *All About Ah-long*, way back in 1989, but for a long time now his films have largely eschewed melodrama. Perhaps the downbeat ambience of *PTU* and its strangely deflated ending reflected a new questioning critical mood among Hong Kong people who were disenchanted with the idea of 'heroes' and who felt cynical about the Hong Kong government's patronising grand narratives. In her film *Ordinary Heroes* (1999), veteran fellow-director Ann Hui tried to introduce the concept of the unrecognised heroism of ordinary people, who worked to improve the quality of life in the city because that was what their consciences impelled them to do — a very different conception of 'heroic bloodshed'. The doctors and nurses who perished in the SARS epidemic were, for example, treated as heroes, but their heroism was only necessary because of the government's pusillanimity in its dealings with the Mainland.

To's use of deadpan humour, irony and understated farce in the film supports his anti-heroic position, although much of the black comedy is related to absurdity and fate. Borrowing the concept from one of his subsequent films, when we 'run on karma' our fate is pre-destined. This karmic or fatalistic view suggests the underlying sense that life's comedy of errors and coincidences is fated to happen. *PTU* expresses such a position in its representation of incongruity, synchronicity and dramatic irony. The absurd is of course closely connected with a very different kind of philosophy from the Asian ones of *Running on Karma*, namely existentialism. Do we detect existentialist leanings on the part of the director in respect of his characters and in the absurd misunderstandings and coincidences that bring about *PTU*'s muted conclusion? His characters in this and other films such as *Breaking News* must be resigned to expecting the unexpected, since man is unable to control the universe or even the immediate environment. Long stretches of inertia and triviality are followed by sudden explosive and potentially life-threatening action. The cops and gangsters have no time to think, only to react to events and circumstances beyond their control. What man is at liberty to control is the narrative spin on completed events, since history, we are told, is normally written by the winners.

Form, gender and genre: To and the auteur debate

Latterly Johnnie To movies tend to leave more questions unanswered than answered. As he sees it, his films propose a situation for film audiences to reflect on. There is no easy solution and he wants his viewers to continue thinking after they exit the cinema or switch off the DVD player. This is somewhat akin to Brechtian theatre principles, which inhibit cathartic empathy with protagonists and closure in favour of an injunction to audiences to seek possible solutions for themselves. To appears happy that, although people did not originally know what to make of the film, it is now gaining greater appreciation via the festival circuit and the transfer to high quality, anamorphic widescreen DVD. In his study of To's development as a filmmaker of importance, Stephen Teo examined the formalist abstract quality of *PTU* and some of To's other 'exercises':

> *The Mission*, *PTU* and *Breaking News* are graced with outstanding sequences which show To evolving his approach to genre. To is the active agent of genre evolution in which we see a 'gradual shift

> in narrative emphasis from social value to formal aesthetic value'. Such a shift also means that in some respects, the three formalist films are flawed works by dint of the fact that they are 'exercises'. They seem pat and therefore constrained.[3]

Teo's assessments of these 'exercise films' reveals a taste and affection for earlier examples of To's work, which I do not share to the same extent. My own preference — and this is very much a matter of individual taste — is, as the reader will have discerned by now, for his output of the post-97 years. The other problem about genre categorisation is that *PTU* is only very marginally an action film; to be accurate it is much more a crime or *policier* work. Stylish and stylised and yet quite realistic too, the film falls between the cracks of genre. Teo makes a distinction between what he describes as the filmmaker's minor and major work. He also makes a fascinating, and I think illuminating, comparison between To's filmmaking and the Hollywood old studio system filmmakers like Howard Hawks, John Ford and Raoul Walsh, 'who were able to churn out minor and major films as a matter of course'.[4] The stylistic, genre-crossing characteristics of *PTU* qualify it as a major work artistically, even though the film was not a major money-earner for To at the box office.

To's idiosyncratic approach to form and genre is generally considered the hallmark of the auteur filmmaker. Few Hong Kong filmmakers are thought of, or think of themselves, as 'auteurs'. For many the designation of auteur would be tantamount to box-office poison. The appellation 'auteur' is in any case problematic since just what criteria we apply to call one director an auteur and another just an ordinary director have never been satisfactorily addressed. 'La politique des auteurs', literally, 'authors' policy' is essentially 'the idea that a single person, most often the director, has the sole aesthetic responsibility for a film's form and content', to quote David Cook.[5] Teo's use of the term in relation to To's work is stimulating but ultimately misleading, since it does not clearly define rigorous criteria for auteurship in respect of To's body of work. His critique of To's formalism seems closely linked to his comments on what he sees as the uneven quality of the filmmaker's output. Significantly, To shies away from using the term in discussing his own work, not out of false modesty, I believe, but because whilst most people would probably accept the designation of Bergman, Hitchcock or Kurosawa as auteur filmmakers, recognising their uniquely personal style, it is not a categorisation that he appears to find particularly significant for himself. David Bordwell has used the term with reference to action director John Woo, whose films he calls 'exaggeratedly distinctive, caricaturally personal' and made the point that auteur directors can be categorised as those who 'display a consistency of theme and technique from film to film'.[6] By contrast, Gina Marchetti in her study of the Hong Kong film trilogy *Infernal Affairs* persuasively argues for a critical rethinking of the term in relation to recent Hong Kong cinema: 'The "auteur" functions less as an "author" and more as a "brand" with a "name" as the guarantee of a specific market niche. Part of the rise of the co-directed, international blockbuster (e.g. films by the Coen brothers, the Wachowski brothers, Johnnie To/Wai Ka-fai), *Infernal Affairs* moves beyond the personal film and the obsessions of a single auteur into a creative environment, which revolves around anti-individualism and eclecticism.'[7]

Although To's recent cinema could be said to exhibit quasi-auteurist tendencies, I do not believe that it is very productive to deliberate for too long on the classification. Teo's 'uneven auteur' tag admittedly draws useful attention to the heterogeneity of styles evident in To's catalogue, and his critical preference for privileging the so-called 'action films' places To's films within a familiar Hong Kong bracket. However, To himself reacted rather blankly, I thought, when the notion of 'uneven auteur' was put to him in interview. 'It depends how you gauge what is even,' he mused. (See Appendix.) He seemed to think, not unreasonably, that his body of work is his body of work, period. As for the term 'auteur', borrowed from the fifties' *Cahiers du Cinema* theorists as it has been, it may already be past its sell-by date nowadays. In the wake of robust postmodern critiques by Jameson and others, the appropriateness of authorship in the context of such a collaborative medium as cinema may no longer be very apposite.[8] Roland Barthes has in any case mischievously challenged the notion of authorship entirely, attributing the creation of meaning primarily to the receiver/audience.[9] On reflection one cannot help feeling that the art-house associations of the word and its intellectual connotations sit better with a Wong Kar-wai than a Johnnie To. The latter recognises that, while Milkyway Image as an institution affords him greater creative autonomy than he enjoyed at an earlier stage of his career, making claims for one's work as high art is likely to be dismissed as pretentious in the pragmatic Hong Kong film milieu. Perhaps it is legitimate in retrospect to apply the designation 'genre auteur' to Alfred Hitchcock, and it seems to me to serve as a useful analogy with To's body of work, without wishing to compare the latter too closely to that of the 'master' of cinematic suspense. In any event it is evident that To's films display 'a consistency of theme and technique from film to film', the alternating comedic and serious impulses in his output notwithstanding.

By the same token, much of what I have discussed in this and previous chapters makes it clear that the perceived genre shift toward strict aesthetic formalism that Teo claims for *PTU* is not supported by a close analysis of the movie itself. Whilst there is a move toward a more rigorous and distanced aesthetic in *PTU*, the film is also rich in socio-political meanings and implications. Granted, the structural oppositions of conventional genre theory are evident in this film, as they are in most of To's works, but structure and content, form and meaning are here beautifully balanced. The director's original intention was to focus on the relationship between the four main characters, as emblematic of their respective organisations — Lo, Mike, Inspector Leigh Cheng and Baldhead. Obviously there is a sense of symmetry in that they represent four different groups: the Anti-Crime Division (OCTB), the PTU, the CID and the triads. As it happens, the gender balance of two males plus two females — unusual for a Johnnie To non-comedy film — makes Sergeant Kat the fourth member of the quartet, which upsets the group symmetry, since both Kat and Mike are PTU sergeants. In the end the gender balance of Kat in potential opposition to Mike and Leigh Cheng competing with Lo provides a more satisfying symmetrical structure. As To pointed out himself in interview, Lo and Madam are equally stubborn and complement each other perfectly. In spite of To's use of such structural oppositions, the film never feels contrived or calculatedly formal, mainly because the formal properties, far from being 'pat', are so skilfully integrated into the narrative weft of the film. As a result, To's formalistic exercise approach enhances the film's style and content rather than detracting from them.

To's ambivalent slant on gender and genre in *PTU* and the follow-up, *Breaking News*, makes it difficult to pigeon-hole his underlying intentions or the finished work. A misogynist construction of the female gender can certainly be read into both films. Inspector Leigh Cheng, who may be seen as a prototype for the more central Kelly Chen figure (Superintendent Rebecca Fong) in *Breaking News*, is not permitted her triumph over the rule-bending male colleagues in *PTU*, and is even humiliated for her pains. By contrast the steadfast Sergeant Kat not only protects Mike, and by extension Lo, against her better judgment, she acquits herself as well as Mike and acts as a role model to her subordinates in the shoot-out. In *Breaking News* Rebecca Fong's over-confidence in manipulating the media and over-ruling her more street-wise colleagues nearly proves fatal to her personally. To's 'exercise films', then, begin to envisage women as protagonists on the same footing as the men. In the context of public organisations these films depict cross-gender antagonism, but ultimately also a desire for respectful co-existence. Subsequent triad films, notably *Election* and *Exiled*, seemed to have dispensed with the strategy, but the central role for the female rookie in *Eye in the Sky* (admittedly not To's solo project) shows a return to gender balance in the lead roles. It has to be said that, although he has directed many of Hong Kong's leading ladies over the years, To gives the impression of being a lot more comfortable representing the male perspective on life.

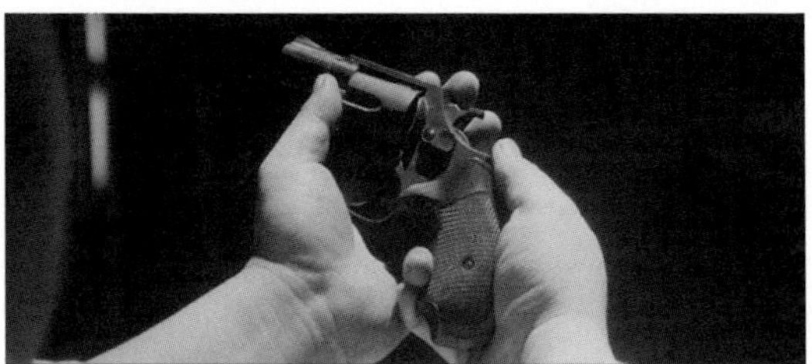

Still 25 Loss of gun/phallus! Recovery of same!

From the standpoint of feminism and also of psychoanalysis, *PTU* reflects a palpable sense of discomfort on the part of older Hong Kong males concerning the ascendancy of women in the city's professional, social and political life. The relentless Madam, for example, dominates her underlings as well as her young informer, and also wants to dominate and catch out the hapless Lo. Indeed, the lady inspector is depicted as his nemesis up to the film's finale, but the 'fat man' has the last laugh. As for macho Mike Ho, he defends the interests of his male colleague, but for Sergeant Kat professional solidarity wins out over gender solidarity. The gun is, of course, sometimes seen as a phallic symbol in cinema and in this film its symbolism is central. Lo's anxiety about the loss of his weapon can certainly be construed psychoanalytically. In general the film expresses a certain fear and distrust of the highly ranked female (as evident also in *Breaking News*), which in turn may well have reflected real-life concerns over the role of 'iron lady' Regina Yip in the Article 23 affair. (As a key member of former Chief Executive Tung Chee-hwa's administration, Regina Yip was given the thankless task of attempting to introduce anti-subversion legislation in Hong Kong in the stormy year of 2003. The unpopular legislation has been shelved for the time being.) Like Madam, the implacable Yip had to back down and eventually resigned from the government. At the time of writing she has already made her inevitable return to Hong Kong politics, having contested a district council election with another redoubtable lady, Anson Chan, in a close-fought election won by the latter. In interview Johnnie To has quietly expressed his dislike for the high-handed behaviour of senior government officials and his concerns about the future of freedom of speech in Hong Kong. Certainly in *PTU*, solidarity and closed ranks can be viewed as a positive social outcome or from a more ambivalent, even dissident, perspective.

A final example of the fine balance between form and meaning in this shrewdly crafted film is its deft representation of the tension that exists between the desire of the collective and that of the individual. Its world, like the gangster-cop world of Melville, is a sociological and philosophical microcosm of the wider society. Issues surrounding Hong Kong's cultural hybridity and competing mind-sets — Western-style individualism versus Confucian Chinese collectivism — can certainly be read into *PTU*, as can the whole question of the mainland's intervention in the city's cultural and political life. This is too big a subject to be fully explored in the context of the present study, but To's film consciously marginalises the mainland desperadoes, representing them as the alien 'other' disrupting normal business in the Territory. Unity among Hongkongers is of course ultimately achieved in the gunfight against the mainland gang, while the local gangsters are left to fight it out between themselves. Another level of symbolism can be discerned in the interaction between individuals — especially Lo after he loses his gun and his swagger, but also minor characters like the CID informer — and groups, namely the PTU patrols, the CID team and the triad gangs. It is only when the individual becomes isolated, like Lo, Ponytail or the triad bosses in the last part of the film, that they become vulnerable targets. Thus the movie's formalism helps to convey both the random uncertainty of life and the necessity for group identity and allegiance to social structures. Life is not scripted or entirely pre-determined, even if fate does play an important hand, and this explains why the actors were not provided with a completed script, but rather encouraged to improvise around the situations and react more authentically to circumstances. This accounts for the movie's succinct, almost curt dialogue, which both mirrors typically functional Hong Kong–style intercourse and allows more emphasis to be placed on visual elements.

Postscript: 'Johnnie be good'

To is clearly a very good director whose variegated output reflects a keen awareness of milieu, not just of cinematic aesthetics. He is on record as referring to *PTU* as 'a film with his own personal stamp, not that of others', one in which he paid attention to his own vision and not the expectations of the public. For him the aim is always to turn in a good film that meets the criteria he has set himself within the allocated budget.[10] In that sense he is an utterly professional director and, moreover, one with something to say. Whether we interpret *PTU* from a social utilitarian viewpoint and consider To's socio-political intervention as a qualified endorsement of the law enforcement agencies, or following Teo's take on the film, relate its codes and meanings to aesthetic, formal qualities, there is no doubt that the film excites interest and curiosity. Is Johnnie To the mainstay of the film industry, the man to represent Hong Kong overseas in the manner of a cultural ambassador? Or is he a free-spirited, closet critic of an increasingly authoritarian, paternalistic political administration, making dark aspersions about the grand narratives of government? And perhaps most pertinently, will his films continue to resist assimilation into a more positivist and cooperative discourse vis-à-vis the Mainland?

Without question, his films offer sharp postmodern perspectives on Hong Kong society and culture. They transcend the postmodern, hedonistic pop culture and propound a more philosophical perspective on social responsibility and public service ethics. In his personal films, To's down-to-earth, albeit disenchanted, belief in social order does not disguise the fact that he is also critical of the socio-political platitudes of current Hong Kong and mainland politicians and media. Yet his study of the working methods of the PTU is also predicated on Hong Kong's anti-corruption ideals as enshrined in its Independent Commission Against Corruption (ICAC), ideals that are of course very hard to live up to. Clearly Hong Kong has no monopoly on cynical methods for extracting information in this post-Guantanamo era, in which the torture of potential informers to obtain the desired information and illegal practices, such as rendition, has been tolerated at the highest political and international levels. These methods have always been with us. It is just that the politicians of every stamp want to make us believe that the business is somehow 'cleaner' nowadays. In that sense the film's potential meanings and references are truly global. The politicians protect themselves, while telling the public that they are protecting us. So we really cannot be surprised that the police's mandate to protect us (according to the dictates of the politicians) is subordinate to their own instinct for self-protection. It is all one big protection racket — this is the subtly subversive implication of *PTU* and, indeed, of other recent To films. Is Johnnie being naughty or good in adding layers of understated critical commentary that relate to sensitive contemporary issues in his films? I leave that up to the readers and viewers to decide for themselves.

Nevertheless, before concluding this study, it is desirable to underline just why *PTU* will remain in the forefront of Hong Kong cinema, among its best films of the past thirty years. Hong Kong's 'plague year' of 2003, its *annus horribilis* so to speak, is now becoming a more distant memory with each passing year, so topicality is not the reason for the film's capacity to endure. The film's strengths are in its creation of mood and atmosphere, its temporal compression, its downplayed but finely judged acting performances, its adroit use of camera and location, its darkly humorous and ironic style and subtext, its ensemble production values, its aesthetically satisfying post-production work and canny direction. But these are, of course, qualities shared by certain other Hong Kong films. Teo's point, which is referenced at the opening of this chapter, about To's idiosyncrasy, consisting of the constant urge to renew himself and reject his own norms, offers a clue to what makes *PTU* a film that continues to speak to us. The spirit of restless scepticism, of socio-political agnosticism, but of commitment to some sort of social code, flawed as it may be, that infuses the film is recognisably Hong Kong. Johnnie To's achievement in *PTU*, a lasting achievement in all probability, is his recognition of our pragmatically motivated Hong Kong virtues as stemming from the same source as our pragmatically motivated vices. The superheroes of Hong Kong genre films and globalised epics are brought down to earth and made human, all too human, in To's sobering vision. Together with the *Infernal Affairs* trilogy, but in a more low-key, slyly humorous idiom than these three blockbusters, *PTU* reinvents the Hong Kong film for the new millennium.

Notes

Chapter 1 Introducing the Film; Introducing Johnnie — 'One of Our Own'

1. E. Cheung and J. Ku, 'Gendered and Sexualized Bodies in Hong Kong Cinema' in E. Cheung and Y. W. Chu (eds.) *Between Home and World, A Reader in Hong Kong Cinema*. Oxford University Press, 2004, 408–9.
2. A. Abbas, 'Hong Kong as a Para-site' in M. Hjort and D. Petrie (eds.) *The Cinema of Small Nations*. Edinburgh: Edinburgh University Press, 2007, 117.
3. K. C. Lo, 'Transnationalisation of the Local in a Circular Structure' in K. C. Lo, *Chinese Face/Off — The Transnational Popular Culture of Hong Kong*. Hong Kong: Hong Kong University Press, 2005, 106.
4. Yiu Wai Chu, 'Hybridity and G(local) Identity in Postcolonial Hong Kong Cinema' in S. H. Lu and Y. Y. E. Yueh (eds.), *Chinese-Language Film — Historiography, Poetics, Politics*. Honolulu: University of Hawaii Press, 2005, 324.
5. P. Willemen, 'Action Cinema, Labour Power and the Video Market' in M. Morris et al. (eds.) *Hong Kong Connections: Transnational*

Imagination in Action Cinema. London: Duke University Press & Hong Kong: Hong Kong University Press, 2005, 223–47.

6. Interview with Miles Wood in M. Wood, *Cine East: Hong Kong Cinema through the Looking-Glass*. London: FAB Press, 1998, 121.
7. Interview with Stephen Teo in S. Teo, *Director in Action—Johnnie To and the Hong Kong Action Film*. Hong Kong: Hong Kong University Press, 2007.
8. Interview with Shirley Lau, *South China Morning Post*, May, 2003.
9. E. Cheshire, and J. Ashbrook, *Joel and Ethan Coen*. Pocket Essential Film, 2002, 8.
10. P. Fonoroff, *South China Morning Post*, 1.5.2003.
11. TJ review in *Time Out*, 4–10 July 2007.
12. Ibid.
13. 27th Hong Kong International Film Festival booklet, 8–23 April 2003, 13.
14. John Woo quoted in interview in Karen Fang's study of John's Woo *A Better Tomorrow*. Hong Kong: Hong Kong University Press, 2004.
15. 'Et voilà. Maintenant le ressort est bandé. Cela n'a plus qu'à se dérouler tout seul ... Après, on n'a plus qu'à laisser faire ... Cela roule tout seul.' J. Anouilh, *Antigone*. Paris: Editions de la Table Ronde, 1946, 54.
16. S. Teo, *Director in Action*, 11.
17. D. Bordwell, 'Transcultural Spaces' in *Chinese-Language Film*, 148.
18. D. Bordwell, *Planet Hong Kong — Popular Cinema and the Arts of Entertainment*. Cambridge, Mass. & London: Harvard University Press, 2000, 246.
19. S. Teo, Keynote speech in Conference on The Film Scene: Cinema, The Arts and Social Change, University of Hong Kong, April, 2005.
20. J. To in interview with the author, 20 August 2007.
21. D. Bordwell, *Planet Hong Kong*, 131.

Chapter 2 'Into the Perilous Night' — Police and Gangsters in the Hong Kong Mean Streets

1. A. Abbas, *Hong Kong Culture and the Politics of Disappearance*. Hong Kong: Hong Kong Unversity Press, 1997, 23.

2. L. Pun, 'The Emotional Map of Hong Kong Cinema' in @LOCATION, 75.
3. L. Pun, 'The Emotional Map', 77.
4. S. Teo, *Director in Action*, 129.
5. A. Abbas, *Hong Kong Culture*, 76.
6. S. Teo, *Director in Action*, 114.
7. A. Abbas, *Hong Kong Culture*, 78.
8. N. Law, report in *South China Morning Post*, 9 July 2006.
9. S. Teo, *Director in Action*, 9.
10. Hong Kong Police government website.

Chapter 3 'Expect the Unexpected' — PTU's Narrative and Aesthetics

1. D. Bordwell, 'Transcultural Spaces' in *Chinese Language Film*, 147.
2. S. Teo, *Director in Action*, 130.
3. E. Knörer, 'Ein Meisterwek der Konzentration' ('A masterpiece of concentration'), *Jump Cut*, http:// www.jump-cut.de/filmkritik-ptu.html/.

Chapter 4 The Coda: What's the Story? — Morning Glory!

1. Translated version from 'Highlights from the Johnnie To interview on the *PTU* DVD', http://www.hkentreview.com/2003/features/jtptu.html.
2. B. Walsh, *Time Asia*, 12 May 2003.
3. S. Teo, *Director in Action*, 143.
4. S. Teo, ibid., 146.
5. D. Cook, *A History of Narrative Film*, 3rd edition. New York: W. W. Norton, 1981, 971.
6. D. Bordwell, *Planet Hong Kong*, 98.
7. G. Marchetti, *Andrew Lau and Alan Mak's* Infernal Affairs – The Trilogy. Hong Kong: Hong Kong University Press, 2007, 164.
8. D. Bordwell, *Planet Hong Kong*.

9. R. Barthes. 'The Death of the Author' in *Image, Music, Text*. Fontana/Collins, 1977, 142–48.
10. Interview for Jean-Pierre Le Dionnet's *Des Films* DVD release of *PTU*.

Appendix: An interview with Johnnie To

Based on a live interview with Johnnie To Kei-fung in Milkyway Image offices, Kwun Tong on Monday, 27 August 2007.

MI: *Stephen Teo refers to you as an 'uneven auteur' in his new book about your work. Is that how you see yourself too? How useful is the description 'auteur' in talking about your body of work?*

JT: When you talk about 'uneven auteur', it depends on what ideas you consider. It's a matter of balance ... whether it is even or uneven. It's about the meaning of this word, right? In my view, this way of dealing with things should not be called 'balanced' or 'even'. It's just that sometimes my work has this particular style but sometimes not, which makes it seem 'uneven'. I don't think you need a ruler to 'measure' if it's even or not. This kind of measurement is not necessary. For audiences who have watched my films after 1996 ... after Milkyway was founded ... they could appreciate this style of mine and Milkyway films. So, what he said might be right, but personally I don't think it should be put that way. Everyone knows what I want to bring out in my films [laughs]. Well, anyway to me, it's simple and I'll give rather a simple answer: at the end, you will have a result.

MI: *If you could make a director's cut of* PTU *would you include a lot more material, or do you think it works perfectly as it is? Is there in fact much more material that didn't make it to the final cut, and were you happy with the formal quality of the film, especially the neat ending?*

JT: Actually *PTU* itself is a complete version. The one [the final cut] you see right now is a complete version, because the editing was done by myself. After I finished the editing of this final cut, that particular version was my idea of how the film should look at that point in time. It's been almost four to five years. If you ask me whether I have a different view or a different angle on this movie now, I would say 'yes'. But it doesn't mean that the message I wanted to talk about has changed. But a few years later at a film festival, I heard from some friends their own views on the film. One of them — the director of the New York Film Festival, a guy named Richard — made a comment which had rather a strong impact on me. What he said was that the ending of the film didn't have to be quite so clear. That encouraged me to reconsider the whole movie ... what it would look like from his [Richard's] point of view. It doesn't mean that I want to change anything from the first version. What I want to talk about has already been included in the film. There is a very important point I realised when I edited the last part of the movie — more than ten minutes, a lot of footage — which was how to tell the ending of the story. It's not easy. Many things happen at the same time. You can place certain things at the beginning or at the end or even in the middle. It would still work fine. It took almost a week for me to find a way, to approach the way of story-telling I was looking for. After I told the story, I felt that was the way I wanted to tell it, and then I felt that the movie was ready to be released. A few years later, suddenly this friend came to me and told me his idea about the ending. I think that's interesting. But this is only an idea, because although it may be interesting to re-edit the film, I find that it is not really possible, since not much of the supplementary footage would be good enough to use.

MI: *I find the ending of the film very theatrical in a number of respects. It's a theatrical ending in the way that all the characters collide. It's about coincidence and synchronicity. Everything comes together and it's part of the beauty of the film that you have this theatrically artificial outcome. In general* PTU *has a theatrical quality — a kind of unity of action, time and place — that I find intriguing. Did you plan it that way? Or did it just come about as a product of the unconventional filming process?*

JT: About the theatrical element of the movie — okay. It is partly because I use strong lighting, so the audiences think it's a stage [theatrical]. There are seven major scenes. I would also like to mention later why I use this scene-by-scene method. Actually, when I did the research, the idea is about the relationship between police officers, who protect each other but sometimes play cool toward each other. I want to catch this feeling. They call it Blue Curtain. The question why you get a theatrical sense from it is related to various factors, including lighting, presentation of the images and so on. I aimed deliberately at this effect from the beginning. I used a lot of wide shots, for example. When you go to see plays in theatres, there are only 'wide shots'. No close-ups.

MI: *Does the depiction of Tsim Sha Tsui have something to do with an imaginary poetic TST rather than the real place? Why did you focus on TST when you had to do the shooting in some locations on Hong Kong side?*

JT: My intention regarding this film … I mean the complete 'look', the image of the film … is to do with the way it is quite composed at a certain level. At the very beginning I tried to use the idea of Chinese painting. There is one thing that is very smart about Chinese painting which is its vagueness. You can never see the whole picture. Clouds could be very close to mountains. Streams could be high enough to reach the clouds. You may not see the whole picture, but you can see a section of it, or get the general 'feeling'. Seeing this point of view and using this method [fog/smoke effect] is common in Hong Kong costume drama. Since the work of King Hu people have always used smoke effects. The most important thing is … we filmmakers know … the real purpose of having smoke effect is to block out things that they don't want audiences to see [laughs] … in order to make the scene to have a sense of instability. Smoke does not appear square or triangular. It spreads itself. Those parts that are hidden by smoke are 'free'. People might think smoke would not spoil the picture. Rather, it gives a taste of something. All in all, you cannot have smoke effect very often. In New York it's not possible to use this method to hide something you don't want to see, right? Maybe sometimes in New York you will have that view. You can see it very clearly in Hong Kong. So if you want some smoke in the picture, then it has to be a ghost movie. It's not real. What I think is … I create a contrast by strong lighting. When taking everything into account … After watching the movie, some Hong Kong audiences complained that it jumped from Kowloon City to Sheung Wan after the characters crossed the road [reference to the jump cut showing tram lines in Sheung Wan after the scene set in Kowloon City hot-pot restaurant]. It doesn't matter where the places are. I'm not trying to present a totally real world or realistic place.

MI: *Some people saw* PTU *as offering an allegory or coded message about Hong Kong during SARS and the dark political night of*

Article 23, etc. (Lam Suet as Tung Chee-hwa, even!) Obviously the film can be enjoyed without this kind of interpretation. However is it valid to see the film as a kind of social and political allegory?

JT: Actually the filming of this movie started earlier than SARS. But when the movie was showing in theatres it was exactly the time that SARS occurred. From my point of view, the government after 1997 ... and also the current government ... most of the time have been something of a problem. Tung Chee-hwa was certainly a fool and that worsened the problem. Now the economy is getting better, but at a certain level, I think freedom of speech has been censored or has been reduced. So to a certain extent I feel subconsciously rebellious against the system and the government, or at least the government's work. You asked whether Lam Suet represents Tung Chee-hwa. I can certainly tell you 'no!' [laughs] If you ask me whether I have added my own opinion into the movie about politics and the government of the Special Administrative Region, I can say 'yes'. The film that really represents this feeling ... it is not related to *PTU* ... the thing that really represents the post-SARS atmosphere, and which gave me the very strong feeling that urged me to make a movie is *Throw Down*. This movie is about changes in society and about a very depressed society. I created that movie because of such a feeling.

MI: *I heard from another interview that there was a lot of improvisation with* PTU *because the script wasn't fixed. Did things work out the way you expected, and were you very happy with the results?*

JT: It was set at the beginning that everything has to be solved by 4 a.m. — in other words, before dawn. The time-frame was established at the beginning of the film. The idea of the story is about things that happen in a seven-to-eight-hour period. But the film was actually shot over a two-year period. I quite enjoyed the process of filming the movie. I mean making movies is about improvising to me. In a way it's pressure-free, which means that everyone sustains interest in the project. As for the actors, they had no idea what I was shooting at the beginning. But I told them my idea and what to do, and they tried to follow it as closely as possible. I mean in the sense, they were discovering things just like the characters are discovering them. They didn't know what was going to happen next. After six months I called the actors back to the movie. They were surprised. They had already forgotten about it. In fact, some of them thought I had abandoned the film.

MI: *How did the Police (and the PTU) react to the film? Did you get any feedback about this? What other feedback did you get about the film and how did you feel about the overall response?*

JT: You mean the audiences or the policemen? It was tragic when the movie was out in the theatres, because Hong Kong was hit by SARS. No one went to the movies at that time. The box-office take for the film was about HK$2 million, so I was relieved about that. The first point is that in the face of such a public crisis, there were some people brave enough to go into theatres, so I guess I do have some fans out there. The second thing is that I felt the movie would not be a mainstream one or a blockbuster film when I was working on it. I remember the box office for *The Mission* was about HK$2 million, which was more or less the same. There was no SARS when *The Mission* was released. The box office was also okay for *Throw Down* and the feedback back then was really good. Many people called me after seeing the movie. I got really good feedback. When the DVD and VCD came out, I could really see that people loved it. And then, there are audiences who are open to this type of film (*Throw Down*, *The Mission*, *PTU*). There is a niche audience and it is not as small as I originally thought. As for the police, the problem you mention did exist. So what's the difference between gangsters and police? The most important point for me was that I did a lot of research suggesting that certain acts of the PTU might not be legal. Or to put it another way, they would resort to their own methods of solving the matter in hand, and not necessarily according to law or justice. When it comes down to what is most important in the film, that element is not central, however. When you look at the way the theme is further developed the central idea is really about the 'Blue Curtain'. The acts of the police force were not the things I wanted to focus on. The basic meaning of the concept of 'Blue Curtain' is about 'officials who protect each other', according to the Chinese saying about protecting your own people. Everyone has to protect each other, no matter what. There is a unique culture about the force which is not known by the public. For example, if you see your colleague collect money from others, or if you see your colleague assault people together with other policemen, you should never stand up and give evidence as an eye witness. That doesn't mean that you necessarily agree with what is done. The meaning of Blue Curtain is about a kind of invisible protection. They have this invisible protection, because they are police officers. It's necessary, because you don't know what your adversary has set up for you. You don't know what the gangsters and bad elements are hiding behind their backs; you can never know if you're not a policeman how difficult these situations are to deal with. Do you understand? I mean, if you implicate your colleague or 'buddy' without thinking, many people will be embroiled in the situation. Even if it's true that someone has been beaten up, as a policeman you should say that it didn't happen, or everyone will get into trouble if you tell. If you see it, but you don't want to get involved, you must say 'I saw nothing' or 'I don't know' but actually you do. You can never say 'I saw my colleague hit someone'. The police hate this kind of person. They think you've betrayed the whole police team. Just like at the end of the movie where Lam Suet [Sergeant Lo] says to the female detective played by Ruby, 'Madam, fire two shots ... for the report.' Up to this point of the film their inter-relationship has been very distrustful and hostile, but at the end, they collude in a lie, because everyone lies. Everyone has to recount the same story of what happened, so they all lie to cover up. That's why the movie is all about their world. When they act in such a way, does it mean that there's no justice? That's my question. Is it that important? Is it correct? I have no solution to this question. I leave it to the audience to judge. The real answer to that question must be that when judged rationally according to the idea of justice, everyone is in the wrong. But in that sense, most interesting films ask more questions than they give answers, and I think that's what makes *PTU* a bit different in the context of Hong Kong. Actually I believe that this type of movie gives the audiences more space to think individually without any simple answer, if I can put it this way. It doesn't need any solution.

MI: *The titles of your films seem to work really well in English. And the films are well positioned for overseas markets. Overseas audiences seem to really like your style. Have you given much thought to the idea of getting more into the overseas markets? And by contrast, how do you think Hong Kong audiences have reacted to the film?*

JT: [Laughs] For the past decades, Hong Kong film producers gave good Chinese names to their film but just made up terrible ones in English. Some of them didn't even care if the audiences understood, for example the street names. In the past decades, Hong Kong movies have entered a different phase, I mean in relation to Western cinema. Some of the Hong Kong directors went to Hollywood. Some of them even won Oscars. I mean that 'the words' have changed. Even Hong Kong people or Chinese people in Asia have tried to improve their English. So now after a number of years there has been a gradual change in Hong Kong's attitude towards the overseas market and overseas movies. But you still need to express what the movie wants to say. I mean you'll make the audiences buy the wrong ticket, if you give the film a title that makes it sound like a comedy, but actually it's a serious film. In such situations audiences would not know what kind of movie it is. They would not even trust the company who promotes the movie. After receiving all this feedback over many years, movie companies in Hong Kong now need to focus more on English titles, I believe.

MI: *The male-female dynamic in* PTU *is rather interesting and symmetrical: Simon Yam and Lam Suet set against Maggie Shiu and Ruby Wong respectively. Is this important or symbolic in your view as director? Were you conscious of achieving a balance that resonates with the kind of symmetry and balance of a more formal approach to filmmaking? Or is it just the way the film worked out through improvisation?*

JT: I decided to have a female detective and a female uniformed officer in the film. There are regulations which must be observed by the police force concerning gender equality. It would be wrong to recruit men only. There must be female police officers, so it would not be very realistic to exclude females. Thus, we have to talk about female officers as well as males in this kind of movie. I didn't do it deliberately to make a point about females. I mean, before I wrote the female characters [Ruby Wong and Maggie Shiu] I also wrote a senior male character – Lam Suet's boss. Anyway the CID superintendent could equally well be male, right? Perhaps it balances the whole film that we cast a female for such a role, but realistically it would also be okay for a man to play this role. As for the Ruby Wong character [Inspector Leigh Cheng] her fault is understandable, compared with a male character that's clumsy, drops his gun and makes other blunders. Generally speaking, you'll forgive the CID inspector's mistakes more easily as she's a woman in the antagonist role.

MI: *Can I just ask you about the concept of action films? John Woo in interview actually said his films are just action films, pure action films. The book by Stephen Teo makes the same point about you. It's called* Director in Action: Johnnie To and the Hong Kong Action Film. *According to you does* PTU *belong to this action category?*

JT: It's not an action movie. Actually, I would put it this way: *PTU* is quite ... a dark cult movie.

MI: *Audiences have, I think, been very positive about the film in Hong Kong.* PTU *was released in the UK* [July 2007] *shortly after* Exiled *came out and had excellent reviews. In fact the response to both films worldwide seems to have been very positive. One or two reviews said that characterisation and plot were a bit underdeveloped. But I think this is a misreading. Maybe there is a gap of understanding between audiences and Hong Kong films in the overseas markets. What do you think?*

JT: In both *Exiled* and *PTU* I think I have put everything I wanted to say into the movies. *PTU* is compressed into events that happen within eight hours. *Exiled* is also about events that happen in a compressed time period — two or three days. Maybe I should put it this way: if they are not satisfied with my film, or they may think it's shallow at a certain level, they may be right, but that's not what I want to talk about. It's not my main focus, I think. Take *Exiled* for example. Why were the characters standing on the street for so long at the opening? Why did the camera hold for so long? Why did the characters take ten minutes to do anything? It's very simple. Because that's the way I like it, so that's the way it is. When I work on a movie, I like to think that it's not about whether the character is good-looking or not. It's about the combination of images and characters, the overall picture, the way of story-telling. The story is simple, perhaps only ten pages long. So why should I make it a ninety-minute movie? But again, this is the way I like it. You have to enjoy the picture and every shot you make. If the audiences like it, they like it. If they don't, that's fine too. I'll have nothing to say. But why I make movies is not about that. I mean, you can never take a ruler to measure it ... whether the elements are enough or not, or in the right proportion. The audiences have a right to make these judgments, considering many elements and details in the movie. There's no right or wrong in people's response.

MI: *Do you see much likelihood of being lured away from Hong Kong to direct in the US or France (you're pretty popular there!) — emulating John Woo, as it were? Would it depend on the project, or do you feel more comfortable staying in Hong Kong with the control that Milkyway Image gives you?*

JT: My answer to this is not related to the previous questions. What I said about the overseas market doesn't correspond to the question of whether or not I want to work in the West or in English-language film. Actually, I have been asked the same question for many years now. What I feel is that movies are a symbolic projection of one's culture. Of course, cinema is also a very creative channel in which to express oneself. But as a creator, I need to understand myself and know in which context I can express all that I want to say freely. It's been nearly two decades since the first director from Hong Kong went to work abroad. I have not yet come to a decision because, as I have said, your own culture and your field of creativity present certain restrictions in the potential expressiveness of your films. These considerations make me hesitate. It goes without saying that any film you make overseas must be different from what you can make in your own cultural context. I don't believe that such a film would either touch or be felt so clearly by audiences. Even if I have the chance to make such a movie today, necessarily it would have to be a commercial undertaking rather than the type of film that I really want to make. After all, commercial cinema is the mainstream. Of course, art films can also make money. In very commercial enterprises you have to consider what the movie company people are thinking about, instead of what you are thinking about. I wonder whether, given more time and space to enter into that mentality, I will try to accept the challenge. You never know: the two approaches — mine and the overseas commercial approach — may get closer over a period of time. Maybe it wouldn't be a matter of having to go to the extreme of producing English-language films in the Hollywood way. I guess, only time will tell!

Grateful thanks to Tiffany Ng, Sharon Chan and Daisy Ng for translation and transcription.

Credits

PTU

Running time: 88 minutes, colour, Cantonese with English subtitles

Director	Johnnie To
Producer	Johnnie To
Screenplay	Yau Nai-hoi and Au Kin-yee from an idea by Johnnie To
Director of Photography	Cheng Siu-keung
Editor/ Associate Director	Law Wing-cheong
Sound Editing	Martin Chappell; Charlie Lo
Music	Chung Chi-wing
Art Director	Jerome Fung
Assistant Director and Continuity	Chan Ho-ming
Post-production Editor	Christy Chan
Production Executive	Catherine Chan
Administrative Producer	Patrick Tong
Production	Milkyway Image HK Ltd.
Distribution	Mei Ah Film Company

Main Cast

Sgt. Mike Ho	Simon Yam
Kat	Maggie Shiu
Sgt. Lo Sa	Lam Suet
Inspector Leigh Cheng	Ruby Wong
Baldhead	Lo Hoi-pang
PTU Rookie	Raymond Wong
Uncle Chung	Wong Tin-lam
Eyeball	Eddy Ko

Awards

23rd Annual HK Film Awards: Winner: Best director (Johnnie To)

40th Golden Horse Awards: Winner: Best original screenplay (Yau Nai-hoi and Au Kin-yee)

Prix du Jury de Cognac (France): 2004

9th Annual Golden Bauhinia Awards (Hong Kong): Winner: Best picture; Best director; Best lead actor (Simon Yam); Best supporting actor (Lam Suet); Best supporting actress (Maggie Shiu); Best original screenplay (Yau Nai-hoi and Au Kin-yee)

Seattle International Film Festival Asian Trade Winds Award (Johnnie To)

Hong Kong Film Critics' Society Award: Film of Merit

DVD editions of *PTU*

Mei-Ah DVD – Cantonese/ Mandarin with English sub-titles. www.meiah.com

Pathé/Des Films (collection dirigée par Jean-Pierre Dionnet) – Cantonese with French sub-titles. Includes presentation of film by J-P. Dionnet and interviews. Site: www.asianstar.fr. No: 457167

Johnnie To Filmography (as director/ co-director)

The Enigmatic Case (1980)
The Happy Ghost 3 (1986)
The Seven Year Itch (1987)
The Eighth Happiness (1988)
All About Ah-long (1989)

The Fun, the Luck and the Tycoon (1990)
Casino Raiders II; *The Story of My Son* (1991)
Justice My Foot; *The Lucky Encounter* (1992)
The Heroic Trio (with Ching Siu-tung); *Executioners* (with Ching Siu-tung); *The Mad Monk* (1993)
Loving You (1995)
A Moment of Romance II (1996)
Lifeline (1997)
A Hero Never Dies (1998)
Where a Good Man Goes; *Running Out of Time*; *The Mission* (1999)
Needing You (with Wai Ka-fai); *Help* (2000)
Fulltime Killer (with Wai Ka-fai) (2001)
Love on a Diet (with Wai Ka-fai); *Running Out of Time 2* (with Law Wing-cheung); *Fat Choi Spirit* (with Wai Ka-fai); *My Left Eye Sees Ghosts* (with Wai Ka-fai) (2002)
Love for All Seasons; *PTU*; *Turn Left, Turn Right* (with Wai Ka-fai); *Running on Karma* (with Wai Ka-fai) (2003)
Breaking News; *Throw Down*; *Yesterday Once More* (2004)
Election I (2005)
Election II; *Exiled* (2006)
Linger; *The Mad Detective* (with Wai Ka-fai); *Eye in the Sky* (as producer/co-director) (2007)
Sparrow (2008)

Bibliography

Abbas, A. *Hong Kong Culture and the Politics of Disappearance*. Hong Kong: Hong Kong University Press, 1997.

Anouilh, J. *Antigone*. Paris: Editions de la Table Ronde, 1946.

Barthes, R. *Image, Music, Text*, trans. Stephen Heath. London: Fontana/ Collins, 1977.

Barthes, R. *The Pleasure of the Text*. London: Jonathan Cape, 1975.

Bordwell, D. *Planet Hong Kong – Popular Cinema and the Arts of Entertainment*. Cambridge, Mass. & London: Harvard University Press, 2000.

Cheshire, E. and Ashbrook, J. *Joel and Ethan Coen*. Pocket Essential Film, 2002.

Cheung, E. and Chu Y. W., eds. *Between Home and World – A Reader in Hong Kong Cinema*. Hong Kong: Oxford University Press (China), 2004.

Cook, D. *A History of Narrative Film*, 3rd edition. New York: W. W. Norton, 1981.

Deleuze, G. *Cinema 1: The Movement Image*, trans. H. Tomlinson and B. Habberjam. London: Continuum, 2005.

Deleuze, G. *Cinema 2: The Time Image*, trans. H. Tomlinson and R. Galeta. London: Continuum, 2005.

Fang, K. *John Woo's* A Better Tomorrow. Hong Kong: Hong Kong University Press, The New Hong Kong Cinema Series, 2004.

Hill, J. and Church Gibson, P. *The Oxford Guide to Film Studies*. Oxford: Oxford University Press, 1998.

Hjört, M. and Petrie, D., eds. *The Cinema of Small Nations*. Edinburgh: Edinburgh University Press, 2007.

Hong Kong Film Archive, @LOCATION Exhibition catalogue, 2006.

Hong Kong International Film Festival, Programme for the 27th Hong Kong International Film Festival, 2003.

Jameson, F. *Postmodernism, or the Cultural Logic of Late Capitalism*. Durham, N.C.: Duke University Press, 1991.

Law K. and Bren, F. *Hong Kong Cinema: A Cross-Cultural View*. Oxford: Scarecrow Press, 2004.

Lo, K. C. *Chinese Face/Off — The Transnational Popular Culture of Hong Kong*. Hong Kong: Hong Kong University Press, 2005.

Logan, B. *Hong Kong Action Cinema*. London: Titan, 1995.

Lu, S. H. and Yueh, Y. Y. E, eds. *Chinese-Language Film — Historiography, Poetics, Politics*. Honolulu: University of Hawaii Press, 2005.

Lyotard, J-F. *The Postmodern Condition*. Manchester: Manchester University Press, 1984.

Marchetti, G. *Andrew Lau and Alan Mak's Infernal Affairs — The Trilogy*. Hong Kong: Hong Kong University Press, The New Hong Kong Cinema, 2007.

Massumi, B. 'Realer than Real: The Simulacrum According to Deleuze and Guattari'. *Copyright*, no. 1, 1987.

Metz, C. *Film Language*. New York: Oxford University Press, 1974.

Morris, M., Li, S. L. and Chan, C. K., eds. *Hong Kong Connections: Transnational Imagination in Action Cinema*. London: Duke University Press & Hong Kong: Hong Kong University Press, 2005.

Teo, S. *Director in Action — Johnnie To and the Hong Kong Action Film*. Hong Kong: Hong Kong University Press, 2007.

Teo, S. *Hong Kong Cinema: The Extra Dimensions*. London: British Film Institute, 1997.

Thompson, D. and Christie, I., eds. *Scorsese on Scorsese*. London: Faber & Faber, 1990.

Tsang, S. *A Modern History of Hong Kong*. Hong Kong: Hong Kong University Press, 2004.

Verne, J. *Around the World in Eighty Days*. London: Penguin, 1986.

Willett, J. *Brecht on Theatre*. New York: Hill and Wang, 1964.

Wood, M. *Cine East: Hong Kong Cinema through the Looking-Glass*. London: FAB Press, 1998.

Websites:

http://www.hkentreview.com/2003/features/jtptu.html (English translated highlights from the Cantonese language DVD interview)

http://www.cinespot.com/hkmreviews/eptu.html

http://www.time.com/time/asia/magazine/article/0,13673, 501030512-449528 (Big Bad Cops – by Bryan Walsh)

http://www.asianfilms.org/hongkong/ptu.html (Awards)

http://www.asia.cinedie.com/en/johnnie_to.htm (In the galaxy of Johnnie To Kei-fung — profile and interview)

http://www.jump-cut.de/filmkritik-ptu.html (German language review)

http://www.cinemavenire.it/magazine/articolistampa.asp?IDartic=2361 (Italian language review of *Mission* and *PTU*)

http://www.kfccinema.com/reviews/action/ptu/ptu.html

http://www.cineasie.com/PTU.html (French website review)

http://www.asianfilms.org/hongkong/ptu.html

http://www.lovehkfilm.com/reviews/ptu.htm

http://www.culturevulture.net/Movies7/PTU.htm

http://www.naturalbornviewers.com/archive/p/ptu/review.htm